THE BRITANNICA GUIDE TO ISLAM

THE FOUNDATIONS OF ISLAM AND ISLAMIC THOUGHT

EDITED BY ARIANA WOLFF

IN ASSOCIATION WITH

ROSEN
EDUCATIONAL SERVICES

Published in 2018 by Britannica Educational Publishing (a trademark of Encyclopædia Britannica, Inc.) in association with The Rosen Publishing Group, Inc.
29 East 21st Street, New York, NY 10010

Distributed exclusively by Rosen Publishing.
To see additional Britannica Educational Publishing titles, go to rosenpublishing.com.

First Edition

Britannica Educational Publishing
J.E. Luebering: Executive Director, Core Editorial
Andrea R. Field: Managing Editor, Compton's by Britannica

Rosen Publishing
Ariana Wolff: Editor   OCT 2 4 2017
Nelson Sá: Art Director
Brian Garvey: Series Designer
Tahara Anderson: Book Layout
Cindy Reiman: Photography Manager
Nicole DiMella: Photo Researcher

Library of Congress Cataloging-in-Publication Data

Names: Wolff, Ariana, editor.
Title: The foundations of Islam and Islamic thought / [editor] by Ariana
   Wolff.
Description: New York, NY : Britannica Educational Publishing, 2018. |
   Series: The Britannica guide to Islam | Includes bibliographical
   references and index.
Identifiers: LCCN 2016053716 | ISBN 9781680486117 (library bound : alk. paper)
Subjects: LCSH: Islam. | Islam—Doctrines. | Islamic philosophy. | Islamic
   ethics.
Classification: LCC BP161.3 .F675 2018 | DDC 297—dc23
LC record available at https://lccn.loc.gov/2016053716

Manufactured in China

Photo credits: Cover, p. 1 Saida Shigapova/Shutterstock.com; p. 9 Blaine Harrington III/Corbis Documentary/ Getty Images; p. 13 Courtesy of the University of Texas Libraries, The University of Texas at Austin; p. 15 istanbul_image_video/Shutterstock.com; p. 20 DEA/G. Dagli Orti/De Agostini/Getty Images; p. 24 mtsyri/Shutterstock.com; pp. 28, 85 Iberfoto/SuperStock; p. 30 World Religions Photo Library/Alamy Stock Photo; p. 33 Pictures from History/Bridgeman Images; p. 35 Zakir Hossain Chowdhury/Barcroft Media/Getty Images; p. 37 © ayazad/Fotolia; p. 45 Art Directors & TRIP/Alamy Stock Photo; pp. 52-53 Library of Congress Geography and Map Division; p. 59 Reuters/Alamy Stock Photo; p. 62 Stereograph Cards/Prints and Photographs Division/ Library of Congress, Washington, D.C. (digital file no. LC-DIG-ppmsca-10663); p. 63 Gurcan Ozturk/AFP/Getty Images; p. 68 Christine Osborne Pictures/Alamy Stock Photo; p. 70 Wellcome Library, London; p. 72 Georgios Kollidas/Shutterstock.com; p. 76 Photos.com/Thinkstock; p. 81 © Pictures from History/The Image Works; p. 88 Godong/Universal Images Group/Getty Images; p. 91 Marie-Lan Nguyen; p. 97 Jesse33/Shutterstock.com; p. 102 Heritage Image Partnership Ltd/Alamy Stock Photo; p. 107 © AP Images; p. 110 George Grantham Bain Collection/Library of Congress, Washington, D.C. (digital file no. cph 3b24436); p. 113 Prakash Subbarao; p. 116 Barry Kusuma/Photolibrary/Getty Images; back cover, pp. 3-7 background design javarman/Shutterstock.com; interior pages border design Azat1976/Shutterstock.com.

CONTENTS

CHAPTER THREE

ISLAMIC THEOLOGY 41

INTRODUCTION

I slam is the second largest of the Abrahamic religions—that is, belief systems centred on the Hebrew patriarch Abraham. The word "Islam" itself means "surrender." It is understood to imply submission to Allah, or God. Its practitioners are known as Muslims, literally those who submit to God. It holds the core beliefs that Allah is a God without rival; that the 6th-century Prophet Muhammad was Allah's last messenger on Earth; and that believers must surrender to the will of Allah.

Islam's primary beliefs are enshrined in the text of the Qur'ān (sometimes spelled Koran in English), a text that Muslims believe was revealed to the Prophet Muhammad by God. Much like Christianity's relationship to Judaism, Islam does not eschew the prophets of its Abrahamic predecessors. Thus, Islamic belief accepts the major prophets of Judaism and Christianity, among them Abraham, Noah, Moses, and Jesus, as its own and recognizes as holy texts the Torah, Psalms, and the Gospel (although not in the forms preserved by Judaism or Christianity). Thus, Muslims see their religion not as a new advent that began with Muhammad, but rather as the complete and final revelation of a faith that existed since the beginning of time.

Historically, Islam originated in the Arabian Peninsula, a peninsular region located in the extreme southwestern corner of Asia. From there, it spread out west across Africa and east into Asia. Before the rise of Islam, several different civilizations lived throughout the region that would become the Islamic World, each with their own practices and beliefs. Among them were Jews, Christians, Zoroastrians, and indigenous Arab polytheists. The Arabian Peninsula, where Islam was born, was separated into several tribes, including the Quraysh, Muhammad's tribe.

Muhammad was born in 570 CE in the city of Mecca and for several years worked as a merchant. By his 30s, he was a respected figure in Mecca, due in part to his deep religiosity and attention to

8

A veiled woman walks before the Abu Darweesh Mosque in Amman, Jordan. Mosques are the houses of worship where the world's estimated 1.5 billion Muslims gather to pray.

prayer. He often would leave the city and retire to the desert for prayer and meditation. During one of these periods of retreat, in the year 610, Muhammad meditated in a cave called al-Ḥirāʾ in the Mountain of Light (Jabal al-Nūr) near Mecca, where he experienced the presence of the archangel Gabriel and the process of the Qurʾānic revelation began.

Written in Arabic, the Qurʾān is composed in rhymed prose, and it was intended to be recited. Its content includes theological statements, laws and morals, stories of the prophets, oracular or prophetic statements, and disputes with other religions. The Qurʾān presents itself as the speech of God, in an elliptical and cyclical manner—without a linear structure.

Although the Qur'ān includes laws, it is not considered a book of laws that must be followed. On the contrary, according to Islamic belief, the meaning of the Qur'ān is not fixed. Therefore, the religion relies on Hadith (in Arabic, Ḥadīth: literally, "report"; a collection of sayings attributed to the Prophet) as a source of social, political, and religious knowledge. Hadith speak of a wider range of issues, expounding upon the laws mentioned in the Qur'ān, as well as sayings and deeds of Muhammad the Prophet. These two sources form the basis of Islamic doctrine and ritual.

After the Prophet's death in 632, there were debates as to who should succeed him and lead the *ummah,* or Islamic community. With time, the Islamic community became fractured based on differences in authority, theology, and practices. Furthermore, Islam has grown to encompass much more than religious doctrine or a societal model; Islamic thought includes the secular philosophy embodied by thinkers such as al-Rāzī and Avicenna as well as great works of literature including the mystical writings of the Sufi poet Rūmī or the tales immortalized in the *Alf laylah wa laylah* (*The Thousand and One Nights*).

Despite being one of the world's largest religions in numbers of followers, Islam is also often misunderstood by outsiders, particularly in the Western world. By understanding its rich theological history and outgrowth from Arabia, new perspectives on Islam can be gleaned, and it can be appreciated for its valuable contributions to theology, philosophy, and the arts.

CHAPTER 1

ISLAMIC DOCTRINE

From the very beginning of Islam, Muhammad inculcated a sense of brotherhood and a bond of faith among his followers, both of which helped to develop among them a feeling of close relationship that was accentuated by their experiences of persecution as a nascent community in Mecca. The strong attachment to the tenets of the Qur'ānic revelation and the conspicuous socioeconomic content of Islamic religious practices cemented this bond of faith. In 622 CE, when the Prophet migrated to Medina, his preaching was soon accepted, and the community-state of Islam emerged. During this early period, Islam acquired its characteristic ethos as a religion uniting in itself both the spiritual and temporal aspects of life and seeking to regulate not only the individual's relationship to God (through conscience) but human relationships in a social setting as well. Thus, there is not only an Islamic religious institution but also an Islamic law, state, and other institutions governing society. Not until the 20th century were the religious (private) and the secular (public) distinguished by some Muslim thinkers and separated formally in certain places such as Turkey.

This dual religious and social character of Islam, expressing itself in one way as a religious community commissioned by God to bring its own value system to the world through the *jihād* ("exertion," commonly translated as "holy war" or "holy

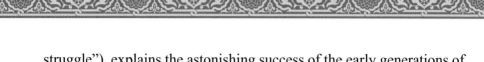

struggle"), explains the astonishing success of the early generations of Muslims. Within a century after the Prophet's death in 632 CE, they had brought a large part of the globe—from Spain across Central Asia to India—under a new Arab Muslim empire.

The period of Islamic conquests and empire building marks the first phase of the expansion of Islam as a religion. Islam's essential egalitarianism within the community of the faithful and its official discrimination against the followers of other religions won rapid converts. Jews and Christians were assigned a special status as communities possessing scriptures and were called the "people of the Book" (*ahl al-kitāb*) and, therefore, were allowed religious autonomy. They were, however, required to pay a per capita tax called *jizyah*, as opposed to pagans, who were required to either accept Islam or die. The same status of the "people of the Book" was later extended in particular times and places to Zoroastrians and Hindus, but many "people of the Book" joined Islam in order to escape the disability of the *jizyah*. A much more massive expansion of Islam after the 12th century was inaugurated by the Sufis (Muslim mystics), who were mainly responsible for the spread of Islam in India, Central Asia, Turkey, and sub-Saharan Africa.

Beside the jihad and Sufi missionary activity, another factor in the spread of Islam was the far-ranging influence of Muslim traders, who not only introduced Islam quite early to the Indian east coast and South India but also proved to be the main catalytic agents (beside the Sufis) in converting people to Islam in Indonesia, Malaya, and China. Islam was introduced to Indonesia in the 14th century, hardly having time to consolidate itself there politically before the region came under Dutch hegemony.

The vast variety of races and cultures embraced by Islam (an estimated total of more than 1.5 billion persons worldwide in the early 21st century) has produced important internal differences. All segments

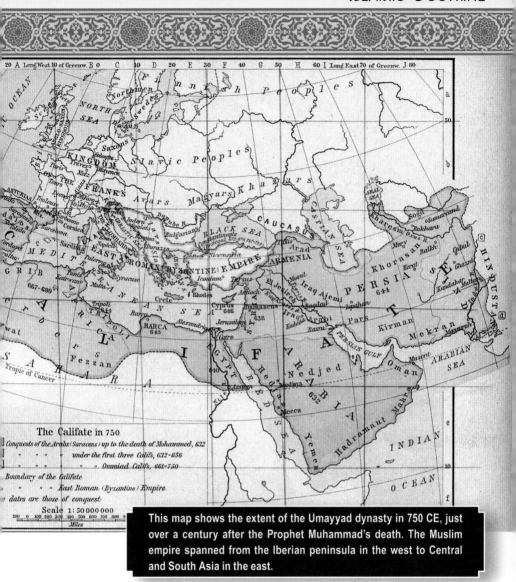

The Califate in 750
Conquests of the Arabs (Saracens) up to the death of Mohammed, 632
            "   "   under the first three Califs, 632–656
            "   "   "   Ommiad Califs, 661–750
Boundary of the Califate
      "   "   East Roman (Byzantine) Empire
• dates are those of conquest
Scale 1:50 000 000
100 0 100 200 300 400 500 600 700 800 9
                 Miles

This map shows the extent of the Umayyad dynasty in 750 CE, just over a century after the Prophet Muhammad's death. The Muslim empire spanned from the Iberian peninsula in the west to Central and South Asia in the east.

of Muslim society, however, are bound by a common faith and a sense of belonging to a single community. With the loss of political power during the period of Western colonialism in the 19th and 20th centuries, the concept of the Islamic community (*ummah*), instead of weakening, became stronger. The faith of Islam helped various Muslim peoples in

their struggle to gain political freedom in the mid-20th century, and the unity of Islam contributed to later political solidarity.

SOURCES OF ISLAMIC DOCTRINAL AND SOCIAL VIEWS

Islamic doctrine, law, and thinking in general are based upon four sources, or fundamental principles (*uṣūl*): (1) the Qurʾān, (2) the Sunnah ("Traditions"), (3) *ijmāʿ* ("consensus"), and (4) *ijtihād* ("individual thought").

The Qurʾān (literally, "reading" or "recitation") is regarded as the verbatim word, or speech, of God delivered to Muhammad by the archangel Gabriel. Divided into 114 suras (chapters) of unequal length, it is the fundamental source of Islamic teaching. The suras revealed at Mecca during the earliest part of Muhammad's career are concerned mostly with ethical and spiritual teachings and the Day of Judgment. The suras revealed at Medina at a later period in the career of the Prophet are concerned for the most part with social legislation and the politico-moral principles for constituting and ordering the community.

Sunnah ("a well-trodden path") was used by pre-Islamic Arabs to denote their tribal or common law. In Islam it came to mean the example of the Prophet—i.e., his words and deeds as recorded in compilations known as Hadith (in Arabic, Ḥadīth: literally, "report"; a collection of sayings attributed to the Prophet). Hadith provide the written documentation of the Prophet's words and deeds. Six of these collections, compiled in the 3rd century AH (9th century CE), came to be regarded as especially authoritative by the largest group in Islam, the Sunnis. Another large group, the Shīʿites, has its own Hadith contained in four canonical collections.

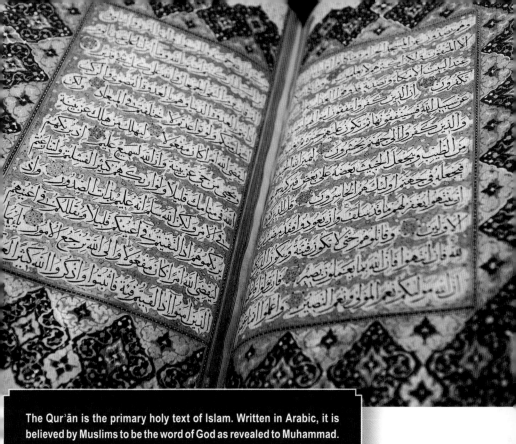

The Qur'ān is the primary holy text of Islam. Written in Arabic, it is believed by Muslims to be the word of God as revealed to Muhammad.

The doctrine of *ijmā*, or consensus, was introduced in the 2nd century AH (8th century CE) in order to standardize legal theory and practice and to overcome individual and regional differences of opinion. Though conceived as a "consensus of scholars," *ijmā* was in actual practice a more fundamental operative factor. From the 3rd century AH *ijmā* has amounted to a principle of stability in thinking; points on which consensus was reached in practice were considered closed and further substantial questioning of them prohibited. Accepted interpretations of the Qur'ān and the actual content of the Sunnah (i.e., Hadith and theology) all rest finally on the *ijmā* in the sense of the acceptance of the authority of their community.

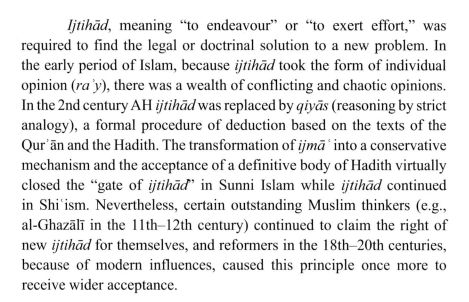

Ijtihād, meaning "to endeavour" or "to exert effort," was required to find the legal or doctrinal solution to a new problem. In the early period of Islam, because *ijtihād* took the form of individual opinion (*ra'y*), there was a wealth of conflicting and chaotic opinions. In the 2nd century AH *ijtihād* was replaced by *qiyās* (reasoning by strict analogy), a formal procedure of deduction based on the texts of the Qur'ān and the Hadith. The transformation of *ijmā'* into a conservative mechanism and the acceptance of a definitive body of Hadith virtually closed the "gate of *ijtihād*" in Sunni Islam while *ijtihād* continued in Shi'ism. Nevertheless, certain outstanding Muslim thinkers (e.g., al-Ghazālī in the 11th–12th century) continued to claim the right of new *ijtihād* for themselves, and reformers in the 18th–20th centuries, because of modern influences, caused this principle once more to receive wider acceptance.

Doctrines of the Qur'ān

As the sacred scripture of a world religion, the Qur'ān contains all the guidance necessary for Muslims, and there is practically no aspect of life with which it does not deal. Above all, the Qur'ān is concerned with the ultimate nature of reality, or God (Allah); Muslims believe that the Qur'ān's exposition of this reality is the most complete possible.

God

The doctrine about God in the Qur'ān is rigorously monotheistic: God is one and unique; he has no partner and no equal. Trinitarianism, the Christian belief that God is three persons in one substance, is vigorously repudiated. Muslims believe that there are no intermediaries between God and the creation that he brought into being by his sheer

command, "Be." Although his presence is believed to be everywhere, he is not incarnated in anything. He is the sole creator and sustainer of the universe, wherein every creature bears witness to his unity and lordship. But he is also just and merciful: his justice ensures order in his creation, in which nothing is believed to be out of place, and his mercy is unbounded and encompasses everything. His creating and ordering the universe is viewed as the act of prime mercy for which all things sing his glories. The God of the Qur'ān, described as majestic and sovereign, is also a personal God; he is viewed as being nearer to one than one's own jugular vein, and, whenever a person in need or distress calls him, he responds. Above all, he is the God of

TAWHID

Tawhid (in Arabic Tawḥīd: "making one," "asserting oneness") refers to the Islamic concept of the oneness of God, in the sense that he is one and there is no god but he, as stated in the *shahādah* ("witness") formula: "There is no god but God and Muhammad is His prophet." Tawhid further refers to the nature of that God—that he is a unity, not composed, not made up of parts, but simple and uncompounded. The doctrine of the unity of God and the issues that it raises, such as the question of the relation between the essence and the attributes of God, reappear throughout most of Islamic history. In the terminology of Muslim mystics (Sufis), however, tawhid has a pantheistic sense; all essences are divine, and there is no absolute existence besides that of God. To most Muslim scholars, the science of tawhid is the systematic theology through which a better knowledge of God may be reached, but to the Sufis, knowledge of God can be reached only through religious experience and direct vision.

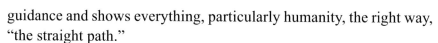

guidance and shows everything, particularly humanity, the right way, "the straight path."

This picture of God—wherein the attributes of power, justice, and mercy interpenetrate—is related to the concept of God shared by Judaism and Christianity and also differs from the concepts of pagan Arabia, to which it provided an effective answer. The pagan Arabs believed in a blind and inexorable fate over which humans had no control. For this powerful but insensible fate the Qur'ān substituted a powerful but provident and merciful God. The Qur'ān carried through its uncompromising monotheism by rejecting all idolatry and eliminating all gods that the Arabs worshipped in their sanctuaries (*harams*), the most prominent of which was the Ka'bah sanctuary in Mecca itself.

THE UNIVERSE

In order to prove the unity of God, the Qur'ān lays frequent stress on the design and order in the universe. There are no gaps or dislocations in nature. Order is explained by the fact that every created thing is endowed with a definite and defined nature whereby it falls into a pattern. This nature, though it allows every created thing to function in a whole, sets limits; and this idea of the limitedness of everything is one of the most fixed points in both the cosmology and theology of the Qur'ān. The universe is viewed, therefore, as autonomous, in the sense that everything has its own inherent laws of behaviour, but not as autocratic, because the patterns of behaviour have been endowed by God and are strictly limited. "Everything has been created by us according to a measure." Though every creature is thus limited and "measured out" and hence depends upon God, God alone, who reigns unchallenged in the heavens and the earth, is unlimited, independent, and self-sufficient.

HUMANITY

According to the Qur'ān, God created two apparently parallel species of creatures, human beings and *jinn*, the one from clay and the other from fire. About the *jinn*, however, the Qur'ān says little, although it is implied that the *jinn* are endowed with reason and responsibility but are more prone to evil than human beings are. It is with humanity that the Qur'ān, which describes itself as a guide for the human race, is centrally concerned. The story of the Fall of Adam (the first man) promoted in Judaism and Christianity is accepted, but the Qur'ān states that God forgave Adam his act of disobedience, which is not viewed in the Qur'ān as original sin in the Christian sense of the term.

In the story of the creation of humanity, the angel Iblīs, or Satan, who protested to God against the creation of human beings, because they "would sow mischief on earth," lost in the competition of knowledge against Adam. The Qur'ān, therefore, declares humanity to be the noblest of all creation, the created being who bore the trust (of responsibility) that the rest of creation refused to accept. The Qur'ān thus reiterates that all nature has been made subservient to humans, who are seen as God's vice-regent on earth; nothing in all creation has been made without a purpose, and humanity itself has not been created "in sport" but rather has been created with the purpose of serving and obeying God's will.

Despite this lofty station, however, the Qur'ān describes human nature as frail and faltering. Whereas everything in the universe has a limited nature and every creature recognizes its limitation and insufficiency, human beings are viewed as having been given freedom and therefore are prone to rebelliousness and pride, with the tendency to arrogate to themselves the attributes of self-sufficiency. Pride, thus, is viewed as the cardinal sin of human beings, because, by not recognizing

The tale of Adam and Eve is shown as illustrated in the 1583 Arabic manuscript *Zubdat-al Tawarikh* (Cream of Histories) by Luqman-i 'Ashuri.

in themselves their essential creaturely limitations, they become guilty of ascribing to themselves partnership with God (*shirk*: associating a creature with the Creator) and of violating the unity of God. True faith (*īmān*), thus, consists of belief in the immaculate Divine Unity and *islām* (surrender) in one's submission to the Divine Will.

SATAN, SIN, AND REPENTANCE

In order to communicate the truth of Divine Unity, God has sent messengers or prophets to human beings, whose weakness of nature makes them ever prone to forget or even willfully to reject Divine Unity under the promptings of Satan. According to the Qur'ānic teaching, the being who became Satan (Shayṭān or Iblīs) had previously occupied

IBLĪS

Iblīs is the personal name of the devil in Islam, probably derived from the Greek *diabolos*. Iblīs serves as the counterpart of the Jewish and Christian Satan. He is also referred to as *ʿadūw Allāh* (enemy of God), *ʿadūw* (enemy), or, when he is portrayed as a tempter, *ash-Shayṭān* (demon).

At the creation of man, God ordered all his angels to bow down in obedience before Adam. Iblīs refused, claiming he was a nobler being since he was created of fire, while man came only of clay. For this exhibition of pride and disobedience, God threw Iblīs out of heaven. His punishment, however, was postponed until the Judgment Day, when he and his host will have to face the eternal fires of hell; until that time he is allowed to tempt all but true believers to evil. As his first demonic act, Iblīs, referred to in

(continued on the next page)

(continued from the previous page)

this context as *shayṭān*, entered the Garden of Eden and tempted Eve to eat of the tree of immortality, causing both Adam and Eve to forfeit paradise. Disguised as the *hātif*, the mysterious voice of Arab mythology, Iblīs also tempted ʿAlī, Muhammad's son-in-law, unsuccessfully trying to keep him from performing the ritual washing of the Prophet's dead body.

Iblīs has long been a figure of speculation among Muslim scholars, who have been trying to explain the ambiguous identification of Iblīs in the Qurʾān as either angel or *jinnī*, a contradiction in terms, as angels are created of light (*nūr*) and are incapable of sin, while *jinn* are created of fire (*nār*) and can sin. Traditions on this point are numerous and conflicting: Iblīs was simply a *jinnī* who inappropriately found himself among the angels in heaven; he was an angel sent to Earth to do battle with the rebellious *jinn* who inhabited the Earth before man was created; Iblīs was himself one of the terrestrial *jinn* captured by the angels during their attack and brought to heaven.

a high station but fell from divine grace by his act of disobedience in refusing to honour Adam when he, along with other angels, was ordered to do so. Since then his work has been to beguile human beings into error and sin. Satan is, therefore, the contemporary of humanity, and Satan's own act of disobedience is construed by the Qurʾān as the sin of pride. Satan's machinations will cease only on the Last Day.

Judging from the accounts of the Qurʾān, the record of humanity's acceptance of the prophets' messages has been far from perfect. The whole universe is replete with signs of God. The human soul itself is viewed as a witness of the unity and grace of God. The messengers of God have, throughout history, been calling humanity back to God. Yet not all people have accepted the truth; many of

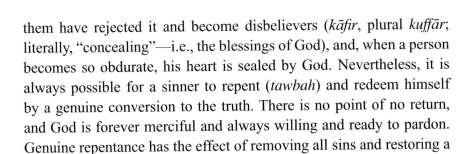

them have rejected it and become disbelievers (*kāfir*, plural *kuffār*; literally, "concealing"—i.e., the blessings of God), and, when a person becomes so obdurate, his heart is sealed by God. Nevertheless, it is always possible for a sinner to repent (*tawbah*) and redeem himself by a genuine conversion to the truth. There is no point of no return, and God is forever merciful and always willing and ready to pardon. Genuine repentance has the effect of removing all sins and restoring a person to the state of sinlessness with which he started his life.

PROPHECY

Prophets are men specially elected by God to be his messengers. Prophethood is indivisible, and the Qur'ān requires recognition of all prophets as such without discrimination. Yet they are not all equal, some of them being particularly outstanding in qualities of steadfastness and patience under trial. Abraham, Noah, Moses, and Jesus were such great prophets. As vindication of the truth of their mission, God often vests them with miracles: Abraham was saved from fire, Noah from the Deluge, and Moses from the pharaoh. Not only was Jesus born from the Virgin Mary, but God also saved him from crucifixion. The conviction that God's messengers are ultimately vindicated and saved is an integral part of the Qur'ānic doctrine.

All prophets are human and never part of divinity: they are the most perfect of humans who are recipients of revelation from God. When God wishes to speak to a human, he sends an angel messenger to him or makes him hear a voice or inspires him. Muhammad is accepted as the last prophet in this series and its greatest member, for in him all the messages of earlier prophets were consummated. The archangel Gabriel brought the Qur'ān down to the Prophet's "heart." Gabriel is represented by the Qur'ān as a spirit whom the Prophet could sometimes see and

23

The Qur'ān narrates the tales of the major prophets of Islam, including Abraham. Shown here is what is traditionally believed to be Abraham's tomb in the Cave of Machpelah in Hebron, West Bank.

hear. According to early traditions, the Prophet's revelations occurred in a state of trance when his normal consciousness was transformed. This state was accompanied by heavy sweating. The Qur'ān itself makes it clear that the revelations brought with them a sense of extraordinary weight: "If we were to send this Qur'ān down on a mountain, you would see it split asunder out of fear of God."

This phenomenon at the same time was accompanied by an unshakable conviction that the message was from God, and the Qur'ān describes itself as the transcript of a heavenly "Mother Book" written on a "Preserved Tablet." The conviction was of such an intensity that the Qur'ān categorically denies that it is from any earthly source, for in that case it would be liable to "manifold doubts and oscillations."

ESCHATOLOGY (DOCTRINE OF LAST THINGS)

In Islamic doctrine, on the Last Day, when the world will come to an end, the dead will be resurrected and a judgment will be pronounced

on every person in accordance with his deeds. Although the Qur'ān in the main speaks of a personal judgment, there are several verses that speak of the resurrection of distinct communities that will be judged according to "their own book." In conformity with this, the Qur'ān also speaks in several passages of the "death of communities," each one of which has a definite term of life. The actual evaluation, however, will be for every individual, whatever the terms of reference of his performance. In order to prove that the resurrection will occur, the Qur'ān uses a moral and a physical argument. Because not all requital is meted out in this life, a final judgment is necessary to bring it to completion. Physically, God, who is all-powerful, has the ability to destroy and bring back to life all creatures, who are limited and are, therefore, subject to God's limitless power.

Some Islamic schools deny the possibility of human intercession but most accept it, and in any case God himself, in his mercy, may forgive certain sinners. Those condemned will burn in hellfire, and those who are saved will enjoy the abiding joys of paradise. Hell and heaven are both spiritual and corporeal. Beside suffering in physical fire, the damned will also experience fire "in their hearts." Similarly, the blessed will experience, besides corporeal enjoyment, the greatest happiness of divine pleasure.

SOCIAL SERVICE

Because the purpose of human existence is submission to the Divine Will, as is the purpose of every other creature, God's role in relation to human beings is that of the commander. Whereas the rest of nature obeys God automatically, humans are the only creatures that possess the choice to obey or disobey. With the deep-seated belief in Satan's existence, humanity's fundamental role becomes one of moral struggle,

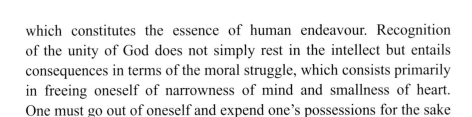

which constitutes the essence of human endeavour. Recognition of the unity of God does not simply rest in the intellect but entails consequences in terms of the moral struggle, which consists primarily in freeing oneself of narrowness of mind and smallness of heart. One must go out of oneself and expend one's possessions for the sake of others.

The doctrine of social service, in terms of alleviating suffering and helping the needy, constitutes an integral part of Islamic teaching. Praying to God and other religious acts are deemed to be incomplete in the absence of active service to the needy. In regard to this matter, the Qur'ānic criticisms of human nature become very sharp: "Man is by nature timid; when evil befalls him, he panics, but when good things come to him he prevents them from reaching others." It is Satan who whispers into a person's ears that by spending for others he will become poor. God, on the contrary, promises prosperity in exchange for such expenditure, which constitutes a credit with God and grows much more than the money people invest in usury. Hoarding of wealth without recognizing the rights of the poor is threatened with the direst punishment in the hereafter and is declared to be one of the main causes of the decay of societies in this world. The practice of usury is forbidden.

With this socioeconomic doctrine cementing the bond of faith, there emerges the idea of a closely knit community of the faithful who are declared to be "brothers unto each other." Muslims are described as "the middle community bearing witness on humankind," "the best community produced for humankind," whose function it is "to enjoin good and forbid evil" (Qur'ān). Cooperation and "good advice" within the community are emphasized, and a person who deliberately tries to harm the interests of the community is to be given exemplary punishment. Opponents from within the community are to be fought and reduced with armed force, if issues cannot be settled by persuasion and arbitration.

Because the mission of the community is to "enjoin good and forbid evil" so that "there is no mischief and corruption" on earth, the doctrine of jihad is the logical outcome. For the early community it was a basic religious concept. The lesser jihad, or holy striving, means an active struggle using armed force whenever necessary. The object of such striving is not the conversion of individuals to Islam but rather the gaining of political control over the collective affairs of societies to run them in accordance with the principles of Islam. Individual conversions occur as a by-product of this process when the power structure passes into the hands of the Muslim community. In fact, according to strict Muslim doctrine, conversions "by force" are forbidden, because after the revelation of the Qur'ān "good and evil have become distinct," so that one may follow whichever one may prefer (Qur'ān), and it is also strictly prohibited to wage wars for the sake of acquiring worldly glory, power, and rule. With the establishment of the Muslim empire, however, the doctrine of the lesser jihad was modified by the leaders of the community. Their main concern had become the consolidation of the empire and its administration, and thus they interpreted the teaching in a defensive rather than in an expansive sense. The Khārijite sect, which held that "decision belongs to God alone," insisted on continuous and relentless jihad, but its followers were virtually destroyed during the internecine wars in the 8th century.

Beside a measure of economic justice and the creation of a strong idea of community, the Prophet Muhammad effected a general reform of Arab society, in particular protecting its weaker segments—the poor, the orphans, the women, and the slaves. Slavery was not legally abolished, but emancipation of slaves was religiously encouraged as an act of merit. Slaves were given legal rights, including the right of acquiring their freedom in return for payment, in installments, of a sum agreed upon by the slave and his master out of his earnings. A slave woman who bore a child by her master became automatically free after her master's death. The infanticide of girls that was practiced

While slavery was not outright forbidden by Islamic law, slaves were given legal rights, and Islam encouraged the release of slaves as a sound moral practice.

among certain tribes in pre-Islamic Arabia—out of fear of poverty or a sense of shame—was forbidden.

Distinction and privileges based on tribal rank or race were repudiated in the Qur'ān and in the celebrated "Farewell Pilgrimage Address" of the Prophet shortly before his death. All are therein declared to be "equal children of Adam," and the only distinction recognized in the sight of God is to be based on piety and good acts. The age-old Arab institution of intertribal revenge (called *tha'r*)—whereby it was not necessarily the killer who was executed but a person equal in rank to the slain person—was abolished. The pre-Islamic ethical ideal of manliness was modified and replaced by a more humane ideal of moral virtue and piety.

chapter 2

FUNDAMENTAL PRACTICES AND INSTITUTIONS

I slam's fundamental practices revolve around core religious and social principles, as embodied in the five pillars of faith. Furthermore, pilgrimage to holy sites of theological significance and the observance of holidays constitute central parts of the Islamic faith.

THE FIVE PILLARS

During the earliest decades after the death of the Prophet, certain basic features of the religio-social organization of Islam were singled out to serve as anchoring points of the community's life and formulated as the "Pillars of Islam." To these five, the Khārijite sect added a sixth pillar, the jihad, which, however, was not accepted by the general community.

THE *SHAHĀDAH*, OR PROFESSION OF FAITH

The first pillar is the profession of faith: "There is no deity but God, and Muhammad is the messenger of God," upon which depends membership in the community. The profession of faith must be recited at least once in one's lifetime, aloud, correctly,

The *shahādah*, or profession of faith, is seen inscribed above the entrance to a mosque. Written in Arabic, it states: "There is no deity but God, and Muhammad is the messenger of God."

and purposively, with an understanding of its meaning and with an assent from the heart. From this fundamental belief are derived beliefs in (1) angels (particularly Gabriel, the Angel of Inspiration), (2) the revealed Book (the Qur'ān and the sacred books of Judaism and Christianity), (3) a series of prophets (among whom figures of Jewish and Christian tradition are particularly eminent, although it is believed that God has sent messengers to every nation), and (4) the Last Day (Day of Judgment).

PRAYER

The second pillar consists of five daily canonical prayers. These prayers may be offered individually if one is unable to go to the mosque. The first prayer is performed before sunrise, the second just after noon, the third in the late afternoon, the fourth immediately after sunset, and the fifth before retiring to bed.

Before a prayer, ablutions are performed, including the washing of hands, face, and feet. The muezzin (one who gives the call for prayer) chants aloud from a raised place (such as a tower) in the mosque. When prayer starts, the imam, or leader (of the prayer), stands in the front facing in the direction of Mecca, and the congregation

stands behind him in rows, following him in various postures. Each prayer consists of two to four genuflection units (*rak'ah*); each unit consists of a standing posture (during which verses from the Qur'ān are recited—in certain prayers aloud, in others silently), as well as a genuflection and two prostrations. At every change in posture, "God

KHUTBAH

Khutbah (in Arabic: Khuṭbah) is the sermon, delivered especially at a Friday service, at the two major Islāmic festivals ('īds), at celebrations of saintly birthdays (*mawlids*), and on extraordinary occasions.

The khutbah probably derived, though without a religious context, from the pronouncements of the *khaṭīb*, a prominent tribal spokesman of pre-Islamic Arabia. The *khaṭīb* expressed himself in beautiful prose that extolled the nobility and achievements of his tribesmen and denigrated the weakness of the tribe's enemies. Even Muhammad presented himself as a *khaṭīb* after taking Mecca in 630. The first four caliphs, the Umayyad caliphs, and the Umayyad provincial governors all delivered khutbahs in their respective areas, though the content of the speeches was no longer strictly exhortatory but dealt with practical questions of government and on political problems and, on occasion, even included direct orders. Under the 'Abbāsids, the caliphs themselves no longer preached but assigned the function of *khaṭīb* to the religious judges (qadis). The pointed insistence of the 'Abbāsids on clearing Islam of the secularism of the Umayyads probably helped strengthen the religious aspect of the khutbah.

is great" is recited. Tradition has fixed the materials to be recited in each posture.

Special congregational prayers are offered on Friday instead of the prayer just after noon. The Friday service consists of a sermon (*khutbah*), which partly consists of preaching in the local language and partly of recitation of certain formulas in Arabic. In the sermon, the preacher usually recites one or several verses of the Qur'ān and builds his address on it, which can have a moral, social, or political content. Friday sermons usually have considerable impact on public opinion regarding both moral and sociopolitical questions.

Although not ordained as an obligatory duty, nocturnal prayers (called *tahajjud*) are encouraged, particularly during the latter half of the night. During the month of Ramadan, lengthy prayers called *tarāwīḥ* are offered congregationally before retiring.

In strict doctrine, the five daily prayers cannot be waived even for the sick, who may pray in bed and, if necessary, lying down. When on a journey, the two afternoon prayers may be followed one by the other; the sunset and late evening prayers may be combined as well. In practice, however, much laxity has occurred, particularly among the modernized classes, although Friday prayers are still very well attended.

THE *ZAKĀT*

The third pillar is the obligatory tax called *zakāt* ("purification," indicating that such a payment makes the rest of one's wealth religiously and legally pure). This is the only permanent tax levied by the Qur'ān and is payable annually on food grains, cattle, and cash after one year's possession. The amount varies for different categories. Thus, on grains and fruits it is 10 percent if land is watered by rain, 5 percent if land is watered artificially. On cash and precious metals it is 2.5 percent.

A crowd of men listen to the Friday sermon (or *khutbah*) in this illustration from a 16th-century copy of the *Dīvān*, a collection of poems by the Persian poet Ḥāfeẓ.

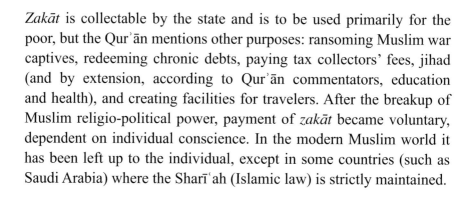

Zakāt is collectable by the state and is to be used primarily for the poor, but the Qur'ān mentions other purposes: ransoming Muslim war captives, redeeming chronic debts, paying tax collectors' fees, jihad (and by extension, according to Qur'ān commentators, education and health), and creating facilities for travelers. After the breakup of Muslim religio-political power, payment of *zakāt* became voluntary, dependent on individual conscience. In the modern Muslim world it has been left up to the individual, except in some countries (such as Saudi Arabia) where the Sharī'ah (Islamic law) is strictly maintained.

FASTING

Fasting during the month of Ramadan (ninth month of the Muslim lunar calendar), laid down in the Qur'ān (2:183–185), is the fourth pillar of the faith. Fasting begins at daybreak and ends at sunset, and during the day eating, drinking, and smoking are forbidden. The Qur'ān (2:185) states that it was in the month of Ramadan that the Qur'ān was revealed. Another verse of the Qur'ān (97:1) states that it was revealed "on the Night of Power," which Muslims generally observe on the night of 27 Ramadan. For a person who is sick or on a journey, fasting may be postponed until "another equal number of days." The elderly and the incurably sick are exempted through the daily feeding of one poor person if they have the means.

THE HAJJ

The fifth pillar is the annual pilgrimage (hajj) to Mecca prescribed for every Muslim once in a lifetime—"provided one can afford it" and

Muslim men gather in a Bangladeshi mosque on the night of 27 Ramadan, known as the "Night of Power" *(Laylat al-Qadr)*. It is believed to be the date when God revealed the Qur'ān to the Prophet Muhammad.

provided a person has enough provisions to leave for his family in his absence. A special service is held in the sacred mosque on the 7th of the month of Dhū al-Ḥijjah (last in the Muslim year). Pilgrimage activities begin by the 8th and conclude on the 12th or 13th. All worshippers enter the state of *iḥrām*; they wear two seamless garments and avoid sexual intercourse, the cutting of hair and nails, and certain other activities. Pilgrims from outside Mecca assume *iḥrām* at specified points en route to the city. The principal activities consist of walking seven times around the Kaʿbah, a shrine within the mosque; the kissing and touching of the Black Stone (Ḥajar al-Aswad); and the ascent of and running between Mount Ṣafā and Mount Marwah (which are now, however, mere elevations) seven times. At the second stage of the ritual, the pilgrim proceeds from Mecca to Minā, a few miles away;

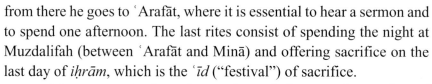

from there he goes to 'Arafāt, where it is essential to hear a sermon and to spend one afternoon. The last rites consist of spending the night at Muzdalifah (between 'Arafāt and Minā) and offering sacrifice on the last day of *iḥrām*, which is the *'īd* ("festival") of sacrifice.

Many countries have imposed restrictions on the number of outgoing pilgrims because of foreign-exchange difficulties. Because of the improvement of communications, however, the total number of visitors has greatly increased in recent years. By the early 21st century the number of annual visitors was estimated to exceed two million, approximately half of them from non-Arab countries. All Muslim countries send official delegations on the occasion, which is being increasingly used for religio-political congresses. At other times in the year, it is considered meritorious to perform the lesser pilgrimage (*'umrah*), which is not, however, a substitute for the hajj pilgrimage.

SACRED PLACES AND DAYS

The most sacred place for Muslims is the Ka'bah sanctuary at Mecca, the object of the annual pilgrimage. It is much more than a mosque; it is believed to be the place where the heavenly bliss and power touches the earth directly. According to Muslim tradition, the Ka'bah was built by Abraham. The Prophet's mosque in Medina is the next in sanctity. Jerusalem follows in third place in sanctity as the first *qiblah* (i.e., direction in which the Muslims offered prayers at first, before the *qiblah* was changed to the Ka'bah) and as the place from where Muhammad, according to tradition, made his ascent (*mi'rāj*) to heaven. For the Shī'ites, Karbalā' in Iraq (the place of martyrdom of 'Alī's son Ḥusayn) and Meshed in Iran (where Imām 'Alī al-Riḍā is buried) constitute places of special veneration where Shī'ites make pilgrimages.

Muslim hajj pilgrims pray as they surround the Ka'bah (the cube-shaped building in the center, and Islam's most sacred site) at the Great Mosque of Mecca, Saudi Arabia.

HOLY DAYS

The Muslim calendar (based on the lunar year) dates from the emigration (*hijrah*) of the Prophet from Mecca to Medina in 622. The two festive days in the year are the Eids (*ʿīds*), Eid al-Fitr, which celebrates the end of the month of Ramadan, and Eid al-Adha (the feast of sacrifice), which marks the end of the hajj. Because of the crowds, Eid prayers are offered either in very large mosques or on specially consecrated grounds. Other sacred times include the "Night of Power" (believed to be the night in which God makes decisions about the destiny of individuals and the world as a whole) and the night of the ascension of the Prophet to heaven. The Shīʿites celebrate

EID AL-FITR AND EID AL-ADHA

Eid al-Fitr (in Arabic, ʿĪd al-Fiṭr: "Festival of Breaking Fast") is the first of two canonical festivals of Islam. Eid al-Fitr marks the end of Ramadan, the Muslim holy month of fasting, and is celebrated during the first three days of Shawwal, the 10th month of the Islamic calendar (though the Muslim use of a lunar calendar means that it may fall in any season of the year). It is distinguished by the performance of communal prayer (ṣalāt) at daybreak on its first day. Eid al-Fitr is a time of official receptions and private visits, when friends greet one another, presents are given, new clothes are worn, and the graves of relatives are visited.

Eid al-Adha (in Arabic, ʿĪd al-Aḍḥā: "Festival of Sacrifice") is the second of the two great Muslim festivals. Eid al-Adha marks the culmination of the hajj (pilgrimage) rites at Minā, Saudi Arabia, near Mecca, but is celebrated by Muslims throughout the world. As with Eid al-Fitr, it is distinguished by the performance of communal prayer (ṣalāt) at daybreak on its first day. It begins on the 10th of Dhu'l-Hijja, the last month of the Islamic calendar, and continues for an additional three days (though the Muslim use of a lunar calendar means that it may occur during any season of the year). During the festival, families that can afford to sacrifice a ritually acceptable animal (sheep, goat, camel, or cow) do so and then divide the flesh equally among themselves, the poor, and friends and neighbours. Eid al-Adha is also a time for visiting with friends and family and for exchanging gifts. This festival commemorates the ransom with a ram of the biblical patriarch Ibrāhīm's (Abraham's) son Ismāʿīl (Ishmael)—rather than Isaac, in Judeo-Christian tradition.

the 10th of Muḥarram (the first month of the Muslim year) to mark the day of the martyrdom of Ḥusayn. The Muslim masses also celebrate the death anniversaries of various saints in a ceremony called ʿurs (literally, "nuptial ceremony"). The saints, far from dying, are believed to reach the zenith of their spiritual life on this occasion.

THE MOSQUE

The general religious life of Muslims is centred around the mosque. In the days of the Prophet and early caliphs, the mosque was the centre of all community life, and it remains so in many parts of the Islamic world to this day. Small mosques are usually supervised by the imam (one who administers the prayer service) himself, although sometimes also a muezzin is appointed. In larger mosques, where Friday prayers are offered, a *khaṭīb* (one who gives the *khuṭbah*, or sermon) is appointed for Friday service. Many large mosques also function as religious schools and colleges. In the early 21st century, mosque officials were appointed by the government in most countries. In some countries—e.g., Pakistan—most mosques are private and are run by the local community, although increasingly some of the larger ones have been taken over by the government departments of *awqāf*.

SHRINES OF SUFI SAINTS

For the Muslim masses in general, shrines of Sufi saints are particular objects of reverence and even veneration. In Baghdad the tomb of the greatest saint of all, ʿAbd al-Qādir al-Jīlānī, is visited every year by large numbers of pilgrims from all over the Muslim world. By the late 20th century the Sufi shrines, which were managed privately in earlier periods, were almost entirely owned by governments and were managed by departments of *awqāf* (plural of *waqf*, a religious endowment). The official appointed to care for a shrine is usually called a *mutawallī*. In Turkey, where such endowments formerly constituted a very considerable portion of the national wealth, all endowments were confiscated by the regime of Atatürk (president 1928–38).

CHAPTER 3

ISLAMIC THEOLOGY

Islamic theology (*kalām*) and philosophy (*falsafah*) are two traditions of learning developed by Muslim thinkers who were engaged, on the one hand, in the rational clarification and defense of the principles of the Islamic religion (*mutakallimūn*) and, on the other, in the pursuit of the ancient (Greek and Hellenistic, or Greco-Roman) sciences (*falāsifah*). These thinkers took a position that was intermediate between the traditionalists, who remained attached to the literal expressions of the primary sources of Islamic doctrines (the Qur'ān, Islamic scripture; and the Hadith, sayings and traditions of the Prophet Muhammad) and who abhorred reasoning, and those whose reasoning led them to abandon the Islamic community (the *ummah*) altogether. The status of the believer in Islam remained in practice a juridical question, not a matter for theologians or philosophers to decide. Except in regard to the fundamental questions of the existence of God, Islamic revelation, and future reward and punishment, the juridical conditions for declaring someone an unbeliever or beyond the pale of Islam were so demanding as to make it almost impossible to make a valid declaration of this sort about a professing Muslim. In the course of events in Islamic history, representatives of certain theological movements, who happened to be jurists and who succeeded in converting rulers to their cause, made those rulers declare in favour of their movements

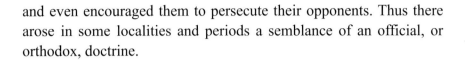

and even encouraged them to persecute their opponents. Thus there arose in some localities and periods a semblance of an official, or orthodox, doctrine.

ORIGINS, NATURE, AND SIGNIFICANCE OF ISLAMIC THEOLOGY

The beginnings of theology in the Islamic tradition in the second half of the 7th century are not easily distinguishable from the beginnings of a number of other disciplines—Arabic philology, Qur'ānic interpretation, the collection of the sayings and deeds of Muhammad (Hadith), jurisprudence (*fiqh*), and historiography. Together with these other disciplines, Islamic theology is concerned with ascertaining the facts and context of the Islamic revelation and with understanding its meaning and implications as to what Muslims should believe and do after the revelation had ceased and the Islamic community had to chart its own way. During the first half of the 8th century, a number of questions—which centred on God's unity, justice, and other attributes and which were relevant to human freedom, actions, and fate in the hereafter—formed the core of a more-specialized discipline, which was called *kalām* ("speech") because of the rhetorical and dialectical "speech" used in formulating the principal matters of Islamic belief, debating them, and defending them against Muslim and non-Muslim opponents. Gradually, *kalām* came to include all matters directly or indirectly relevant to the establishment and definition of religious beliefs, and it developed its own necessary or useful systematic rational arguments about human knowledge and the makeup of the world. Despite various efforts by later thinkers to fuse the problems of *kalām* with those of philosophy (and mysticism), theology preserved its relative independence from philosophy and other nonreligious

sciences. It remained true to its original traditional and religious point of view, confined itself within the limits of the Islamic revelation, and assumed that these limits as it understood them were identical with the limits of truth.

The pre-Islamic and non-Islamic legacy with which early Islamic theology came into contact included almost all the religious thought that had survived and was being defended or disputed in Egypt, Syria, Iran, and India. It was transmitted by learned representatives of various Christian, Jewish, Manichaean, Zoroastrian, Indian (Hindu and Buddhist, primarily), and Ṣābian (star worshippers of Harran often confused with the Mandaeans) communities and by early converts to Islam conversant with the teachings, sacred writings, and doctrinal history of the religions of these areas. At first, access to this legacy was primarily through conversations and disputations with such men, rather than through full and accurate translations of sacred texts or theological and philosophic writings, although some translations from Pahlavi (a Middle Persian dialect), Syriac, and Greek must also have been available.

The characteristic approach of early Islamic theology to non-Muslim literature was through oral disputations, the starting points of which were the statements presented or defended (orally) by the opponents. Oral disputation continued to be used in theology for centuries, and most theological writings reproduce or imitate that form. From such oral and written disputations, writers on religions and sects collected much of their information about non-Muslim sects. Much of Hellenistic (post-3rd-century-BCE Greek cultural), Iranian, and Indian religious thought was thus encountered in an informal and indirect manner.

From the 9th century onward, theologians had access to an increasingly larger body of translated texts, but by then they had taken most of their basic positions. They made a selective use of the translation literature, ignoring most of what was not useful to them until the mystical theologian al-Ghazālī (flourished 11th–12th centuries) showed them the way to study it, distinguish between the harmless and harmful doctrines contained in it, and refute the latter. By this time Islamic theology had coined a vast number of technical terms, and theologians (e.g., al-Jāḥiẓ) had forged Arabic into a versatile language of science; Arabic philology had matured; and the religious sciences (jurisprudence, the study of the Qur'ān, Hadith, criticism, and history) had developed complex techniques of textual study and interpretation. The 9th-century translators availed themselves of these advances to meet the needs of patrons. Apart from demands for medical and mathematical works, the translation of Greek learning was fostered by the early 'Abbāsid caliphs (8th–9th centuries) and their viziers as additional weapons (the primary weapon was theology itself) against the threat of Manichaeism and other subversive ideas that went under the name *zandaqah* ("heresy" or "atheism").

THEOLOGY AND SECTARIANISM

Despite the notion of a unified and consolidated community, as taught by the Prophet Muhammad, serious differences arose within the Muslim community immediately after his death. According to the Sunnis— the traditionalist faction whose followers now constitute the majority branch of Islam—the Prophet had designated no successor. Thus, the Muslims at Medina decided to elect a chief. Two of Muhammad's fathers-in-law, who were highly respected early converts as well as trusted lieutenants, prevailed upon the Medinans to elect a leader who would be accepted by the Quraysh, Muhammad's tribe, and the choice fell upon Abū Bakr, father of the Prophet's favoured wife, 'Ā'ishah. All of this occurred before the Prophet's burial (under the floor of 'Ā'ishah's hut, alongside the courtyard of the mosque).

Al-Ghazālī (flourished 11th–12th centuries)

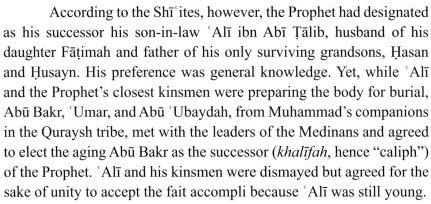

According to the Shīʿites, however, the Prophet had designated as his successor his son-in-law ʿAlī ibn Abī Ṭālib, husband of his daughter Fāṭimah and father of his only surviving grandsons, Ḥasan and Ḥusayn. His preference was general knowledge. Yet, while ʿAlī and the Prophet's closest kinsmen were preparing the body for burial, Abū Bakr, ʿUmar, and Abū ʿUbaydah, from Muhammad's companions in the Quraysh tribe, met with the leaders of the Medinans and agreed to elect the aging Abū Bakr as the successor (*khalīfah*, hence "caliph") of the Prophet. ʿAlī and his kinsmen were dismayed but agreed for the sake of unity to accept the fait accompli because ʿAlī was still young.

After the murder of ʿUthmān, the third caliph, ʿAlī was invited by the Muslims at Medina to accept the caliphate. Thus, ʿAli became the fourth caliph (656–661), but the disagreement over his right of succession brought about a major schism in Islam, between the Shīʿites—those loyal to ʿAlī—and the Sunni "traditionalists." Although their differences were in the first instance political, arising out of the question of leadership, theological differences developed over time.

THE KHĀRIJITES

During the reign of the third caliph, ʿUthmān, certain rebellious groups accused the caliph of nepotism and misrule, and the resulting discontent led to his assassination. The rebels then recognized the Prophet's cousin and son-in-law, ʿAlī, as ruler but later deserted him and fought against him, accusing him of having committed a grave sin in submitting his claim to the caliphate to arbitration. The word *khāraju*, from which *khārijī* is derived, means "to withdraw," and the Khārijites were seceders who believed in active dissent or rebellion against a state of affairs they considered to be gravely impious.

46

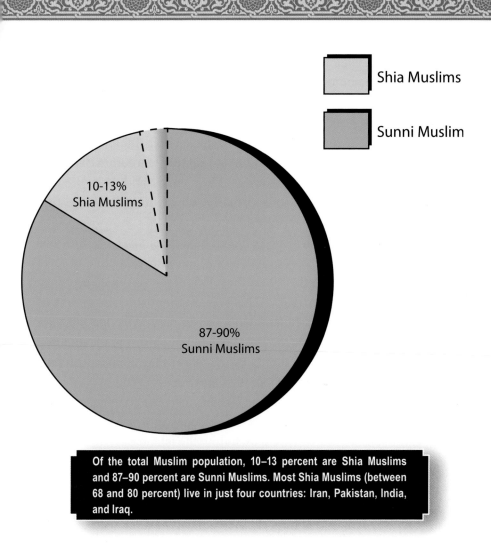

Of the total Muslim population, 10–13 percent are Shia Muslims and 87–90 percent are Sunni Muslims. Most Shia Muslims (between 68 and 80 percent) live in just four countries: Iran, Pakistan, India, and Iraq.

The basic doctrine of the Khārijites was that a person or a group who committed a grave error or sin and did not sincerely repent ceased to be Muslim. Mere profession of the faith—"there is no god but God; Muhammad is the prophet of God"—did not make a person a Muslim unless this faith was accompanied by righteous deeds. In other words, good works were an integral part of faith and not extraneous to it. The second principle that flowed from their

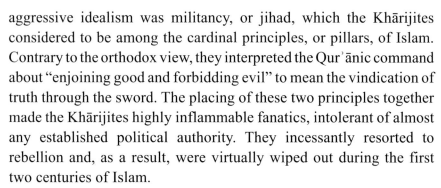

aggressive idealism was militancy, or jihad, which the Khārijites considered to be among the cardinal principles, or pillars, of Islam. Contrary to the orthodox view, they interpreted the Qurʾānic command about "enjoining good and forbidding evil" to mean the vindication of truth through the sword. The placing of these two principles together made the Khārijites highly inflammable fanatics, intolerant of almost any established political authority. They incessantly resorted to rebellion and, as a result, were virtually wiped out during the first two centuries of Islam.

Because the Khārijites believed that the basis of rule was righteous character and piety alone, any Muslim, irrespective of race, colour, and sex, could, in their view, become ruler—provided he or she satisfied the conditions of piety. This was in contrast to the claims of the Shīʿites (the party of Muhammad's son-in-law, ʿAlī) that the ruler must belong to the family of the Prophet and in contrast to the doctrine of the Sunnis (followers of the Prophet's way) that the head of state must belong to the Prophet's tribe, the Quraysh.

A moderate group of the Khārijites, the Ibāḍīs, avoided extinction, and its members are to be found today in North Africa and in Oman and in parts of East Africa, including the island of Zanzibar. The Ibāḍīs do not believe in aggressive methods and, throughout medieval Islam, remained dormant. Because of the interest of 20th-century Western scholars in the sect, the Ibāḍīs became active and began to publish their classical writings and their own journals.

Although Khārijism is now essentially a story of the past, the reaction against it left a permanent influence on Islam. It forced the religious leadership of the community to formulate a bulwark against religious intolerance and fanaticism. Positively, it has influenced reform movements, which sprang up in Islam from time to time and treated spiritual and moral placidity and status quo with a quasi-Khārijite zeal and militancy.

JIHAD

Jihad (in Arabic, jihād: "struggle," or "battle") is a religious duty imposed on Muslims to spread Islam by waging war.

Islam distinguishes four ways by which the duty of jihad can be fulfilled: by the heart, the tongue, the hand, and the sword. The first consists in a spiritual purification of one's own heart by doing battle with the devil and overcoming his inducements to evil. The propagation of Islam through the tongue and hand is accomplished in large measure by supporting what is right and correcting what is wrong. The fourth way to fulfill one's duty is to wage war physically against unbelievers and enemies of the Islamic faith. Those who professed belief in a divine revelation—Christians and Jews in particular—were given special consideration. They could either embrace Islam or at least submit themselves to Islamic rule and pay a poll and land tax. If both options were rejected, jihad was declared.

Modern Islam places special emphasis on waging war with one's inner self. It sanctions war with other nations only as a defensive measure when the faith is in danger.

Throughout Islamic history, wars against non-Muslims, even though with political overtones, were termed jihads to reflect their religious flavour. This was especially true in the 18th and 19th centuries in Muslim Africa south of Sahara, where religio-political conquests were seen as jihads, most notably the jihad of Usman dan Fodio, which established the Sokoto caliphate (1804) in what is now northern Nigeria. The Afghan War in the late 20th and early 21st centuries was also viewed by many of its participants as a jihad, first against the Soviet Union and Afghanistan's Marxist government and, later, against the United States. During that time, Islamic extremists used the theory of jihad to justify violent attacks against Muslims whom the extremists accused of apostasy (Arabic *riddah*).

THE MU'TAZILAH

The question of whether good works are an integral part of faith or independent of it, as raised by the Khārijites, led to another important theological question: Are human acts the result of a free human choice, or are they predetermined by God? This question brought with it a whole series of questions about the nature of God and of human nature. Although the initial impetus to theological thought, in the case of the Khārijites, had come from within Islam, full-scale religious speculation resulted from the contact and confrontation of Muslims with other cultures and systems of thought.

As a consequence of translations of Greek philosophical and scientific works into Arabic during the 8th and 9th centuries and the controversies of Muslims with dualists (e.g., gnostics and Manichaeans), Buddhists, and Christians, a more powerful movement of rational theology emerged. Its representatives are called the Mu'tazilah (literally "those who stand apart," a reference to the fact that they dissociated themselves from extreme views of faith and infidelity). On the question of the relationship of faith to works, the Mu'tazilah—who called themselves "champions of God's unity and justice"—taught, like the Khārijites, that works were an essential part of faith but that a person guilty of a grave sin, unless he repented, was neither a Muslim nor yet a non-Muslim but occupied a "middle ground." They further defended the position, as a central part of their doctrine, that human beings were free to choose and act and were, therefore, responsible for their actions. Divine predestination of human acts, they held, was incompatible with God's justice and human responsibility. The Mu'tazilah, therefore, recognized two powers, or actors, in the universe—God in the realm of nature and humanity in the domain of moral human action.

The Muʿtazilah explained away the apparently predeterministic verses of the Qurʾān as being metaphors and exhortations. They claimed that human reason, independent of revelation, was capable of discovering what is good and what is evil, although revelation corroborated the findings of reason. Human beings would, therefore, be under moral obligation to do the right even if there were no prophets and no divine revelation. Revelation has to be interpreted, therefore, in conformity with the dictates of rationalethics. Yet revelation is neither redundant nor passive. Its function is twofold. First, its aim is to aid humanity in choosing the right, because in the conflict between good and evil human beings often falter and make the wrong choice against their rational judgment. God, therefore, must send prophets, for he must do the best for humanity; otherwise, the demands of divine grace and mercy cannot be fulfilled. Secondly, revelation is also necessary to communicate the positive obligations of religion—e.g., prayers and fasting—which cannot be known without revelation.

God is viewed by the Muʿtazilah as pure Essence, without eternal attributes, because they hold that the assumption of eternal attributes in conjunction with Essence will result in a belief in multiple coeternals and violate God's pure, unadulterated unity. God knows, wills, and acts by virtue of his Essence and not through attributes of knowledge, will, and power. Nor does he have an eternal attribute of speech, of which the Qurʾān and other earlier revelations were effects; the Qurʾān was, therefore, created in time and was not eternal.

The promises of reward that God has made in the Qurʾān to righteous people and the threats of punishment he has issued to evildoers must be carried out by him on the Day of Judgment, for promises and threats are viewed as reports about the future; if not fulfilled exactly, those reports will turn into lies, which are inconceivable of God. Also, if God were to withhold punishment for evil and forgive it, this would be as unjust as withholding reward for righteousness. There can be

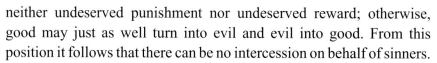

neither undeserved punishment nor undeserved reward; otherwise, good may just as well turn into evil and evil into good. From this position it follows that there can be no intercession on behalf of sinners.

When, in the early 9th century, the ʿAbbāsid caliph al-Maʾmūn raised Muʿtazilism to the status of the state creed, the Muʿtazilah rationalists showed themselves to be illiberal and persecuted their opponents. Aḥmad ibn Ḥanbal (died 855), an eminent orthodox figure and founder of one of the four orthodox schools of Islamic law, was subjected to flogging and imprisonment for his refusal to subscribe to the doctrine that the Qurʾān, the word of God, was created in time.

Sunnism

In the 10th century a reaction began against the Muʿtazilah that culminated in the formulation and subsequent general acceptance of another set of theological propositions, which became Sunni, or "orthodox," theology. The issues raised by these early schisms and the positions adopted by them enabled the Sunni orthodoxy to define its own doctrinal positions in turn. Much of the content of Sunni theology was, therefore, supplied by its reactions to those schisms. The term *sunnah*, which means a "well-trodden path" and in the religious terminology of Islam normally signifies "the example set by the

This map shows the extent of Sunni Islam (represented by light green) in the world today. The smaller region of dark green shading shows the extent of Shia Islam.

Prophet," in the present context simply means the traditional and well-defined way. In this context, the term *sunnah* usually is accompanied by the appendage "the consolidated majority" (*al-jamāʿah*). The term clearly indicates that the traditional way is the way of the consolidated majority of the community as against peripheral or "wayward" positions of sectarians, who by definition must be erroneous.

THE WAY OF THE MAJORITY

With the rise of the orthodoxy, then, the foremost and elemental factor that came to be emphasized was the notion of the majority of the

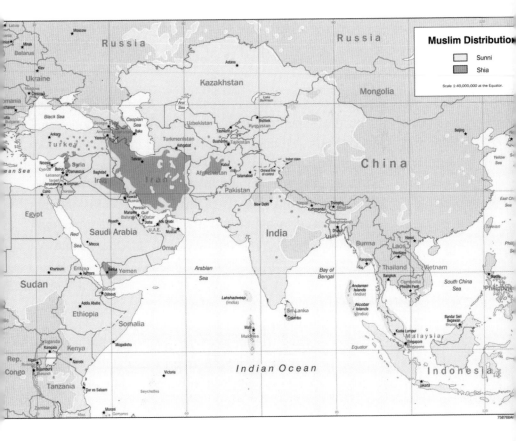

community. The concept of the community so vigorously pronounced by the earliest doctrine of the Qurʾān gained both a new emphasis and a fresh context with the rise of Sunnism. Whereas the Qurʾān had marked out the Muslim community from other communities, Sunnism now emphasized the views and customs of the majority of the community in contradistinction to peripheral groups. An abundance of tradition (Hadith) came to be attributed to the Prophet to the effect that Muslims must follow the majority's way, that minority groups are all doomed to hell, and that God's protective hand is always on (the majority of) the community, which can never be in error. Under the impact of the new Hadith, the community, which had been charged by the Qurʾān with a mission and commanded to accept a challenge, now became transformed into a privileged one that was endowed with infallibility.

TOLERANCE OF DIVERSITY

At the same time, while condemning schisms and branding dissent as heretical, Sunnism developed the opposite trend of accommodation, catholicity, and synthesis. A putative tradition of the Prophet that says "differences of opinion among my community are a blessing" was given wide currency. This principle of toleration ultimately made it possible for diverse sects and schools of thought—notwithstanding a wide range of difference in belief and practice—to recognize and coexist with each other. No group may be excluded from the community unless it itself formally renounces Islam. As for individuals, tests of heresy may be applied to their beliefs, but, unless a person is found to flagrantly violate or deny the unity of God or expressly negate the prophethood of Muhammad, such tests usually have no serious consequences. Catholicity was orthodoxy's answer to the intolerance and secessionism of the Khārijites and the severity of the Muʿtazilah. As a consequence, a formula was adopted in which good works were

recognized as enhancing the quality of faith but not as entering into the definition and essential nature of faith. This broad formula saved the integrity of the community at the expense of moral strictness and doctrinal uniformity.

On the question of free will, Sunni orthodoxy attempted a synthesis between human responsibility and divine omnipotence. The champions of orthodoxy accused the Muʿtazilah of quasi-Magian dualism (Zoroastrianism) insofar as the Muʿtazilah admitted two independent and original actors in the universe: God and human beings. To the orthodox it seemed blasphemous to hold that humanity could act wholly outside the sphere of divine omnipotence, which had been so vividly portrayed by the Qurʾān but which the Muʿtazilah had endeavoured to explain away in order to make room for humanity's free and independent action.

INFLUENCE OF AL-ASHʿARĪ AND AL-MĀTURĪDĪ

The Sunni formulation, however, as presented by al-Ashʿarī and al-Māturīdī, Sunni's two main representatives in the 10th century, shows palpable differences despite basic uniformity. Al-Ashʿarī taught that human acts were created by God and acquired by humans and that human responsibility depended on this acquisition. He denied, however, that humanity could be described as an actor in a real sense. Al-Māturīdī, on the other hand, held that although God is the sole Creator of everything, including human acts, nevertheless, a human being is an actor in the real sense, for acting and creating were two different types of activity involving different aspects of the same human act.

In conformity with their positions, al-Ashʿarī believed that a person did not have the power to act before he actually acted and that God created this power in him at the time of action; and al-Māturīdī

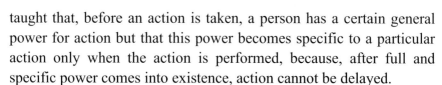

taught that, before an action is taken, a person has a certain general power for action but that this power becomes specific to a particular action only when the action is performed, because, after full and specific power comes into existence, action cannot be delayed.

Al-Ashʿarī and his school also held that human reason was incapable of discovering good and evil and that acts became endowed with good or evil qualities through God's declaring them to be such. Because humanity in its natural state regards its own self-interest as good and that which thwarts this self-interest as bad, natural human reason is unreliable. Independently of revelation, therefore, murder would not be bad nor the saving of life good. Furthermore, because God's Will makes acts good or bad, one cannot ask for reasons behind the divine law, which must be simply accepted. Al-Māturīdī takes an opposite position, not materially different from that of the Muʿtazilah: human reason is capable of finding out good and evil, and revelation aids human reason against the sway of human passions.

Despite these important initial differences between the two main Sunni schools of thought, the doctrines of al-Māturīdī became submerged in course of time under the expanding popularity of the Ashʿarite school, which gained wide currency particularly after the 11th century because of the influential activity of the Sufi theologian al-Ghazālī. Because these later theologians placed increasing emphasis on divine omnipotence at the expense of the freedom and efficacy of the human will, a deterministic outlook on life became characteristic of Sunni Islam—reinvigorated by the worldview of Sufism, or Islamic mysticism, which taught that nothing exists except God, whose being is the only real being. This general deterministic outlook produced, in turn, a severe reformist reaction in the teachings of Ibn Taymiyyah, a 14th-century theologian who sought to rehabilitate human freedom and responsibility and whose influence has been strongly felt through the reform movements in the Muslim world since the 18th century.

SHĪʿISM

Shīʿism is the only important surviving sect in Islam in terms of numbers of adherents. As noted above, it owes its origin to the hostility between ʿAlī (the fourth caliph, son-in-law of the Prophet) and the Umayyad dynasty (661–750). After ʿAlī's death, the Shīʿites (Shīʿah, "Party"; i.e., of ʿAlī) demanded the restoration of rule to ʿAlī's family, and from that demand developed the Shīʿite legitimism, or the divine right of the holy family to rule. In the early stages, the Shīʿites used this legitimism to cover the protest against the Arab hegemony under the Umayyads and to agitate for social reform.

Gradually, however, Shīʿism developed a theological content for its political stand. Probably under gnostic (esoteric, dualistic, and speculative) and old Iranian (dualistic) influences, the figure of the political ruler, the imam (exemplary "leader"), was transformed into a metaphysical being, a manifestation of God and the primordial light that sustains the universe and bestows true knowledge on humanity. Through the imam alone the hidden and true meaning of the Qurʾānic revelation can be known, because the imam alone is infallible. The Shīʿites thus developed a doctrine of esoteric knowledge that was adopted also, in a modified form, by the Sufis. The orthodox Shīʿites recognize 12 such imams, the last (Muhammad) having disappeared in the 9th century. Since that time, the *mujtahids* (i.e., the Shīʿite divines) have been able to interpret law and doctrine under the putative guidance of the imam, who will return toward the end of time to fill the world with truth and justice.

On the basis of their doctrine of imamology, Shīʿites emphasize their idealism and transcendentalism in conscious contrast with Sunni pragmatism. Thus, whereas the Sunnis believe in the *ijmāʿ* ("consensus") of the community as the source of decision making and workable knowledge, the Shī'ites believe that knowledge derived from fallible sources is useless and that sure and true knowledge can come only through a contact with the infallible imam. Again, in marked contrast to Sunnism, Shī'ism adopted the Mu'tazilah doctrine of the freedom of the human will and the capacity of human reason to know good and evil, although its position on the question of the relationship of faith to works is the same as that of the Sunnis.

Parallel to the doctrine of an esoteric knowledge, Shī'ism, because of its early defeats and persecutions, also adopted the principle of *taqiyyah*, or dissimulation of faith in a hostile environment. Introduced first as a practical principle, *taqiyyah*, which is also attributed to 'Alī and other imams, became an important part of the Shī'ite religious teaching and practice. In the sphere of law, Shī'ism differs from Sunni law mainly in allowing a temporary marriage, called *mut'ah*, which can be legally contracted for a fixed period of time on the stipulation of a fixed dower.

From a spiritual point of view, perhaps the greatest difference between Shī'ism and Sunnism is the former's introduction into Islam of the passion motive, which is conspicuously absent from Sunni Islam. The violent death (in 680) of 'Alī's son, Ḥusayn, at the hands of the Umayyad troops is celebrated with moving orations, passion plays, and processions in which the participants, in a state of emotional frenzy, beat their breasts with heavy chains and sharp instruments, inflicting wounds on their bodies. This passion motive has also influenced the Sunni masses in Afghanistan and the Indian subcontinent, who participate in passion plays called *ta'ziyahs*. Such celebrations are, however, absent from Egypt and North Africa.

Although the Shī'ites numbered approximately 130 million of some 1.5 billion Muslims worldwide in the early 21st century, Shī'ism has exerted a great influence on Sunni Islam in several ways. The veneration in which all Muslims hold 'Alī and his family and the

One of the most distinctive features of Shīʿism is the taʿziyah, a passion play reenacting the Battle of Karbalāʾ. Shown is a taʿziyah performed in Nūshābād, Eṣfahān province, Iran, on Dec. 5, 2011.

respect shown to ʿAlī's descendants (who are called *sayyids* in the East and *sharīfs* in North Africa) are obvious evidence of this influence.

Ismāʿīlīs

Besides the main body of Twelver (Ithnā ʿAshariyyah) Shīʿites, Shīʿism has produced a variety of more or less extremist sects, the most important of them being the Ismāʿīlī. Instead of recognizing Mūsā as the seventh imam, as did the main body of the Shīʿites, the Ismāʿīlīs upheld the claims of his elder brother Ismāʿīl. One group of Ismāʿīlīs, called Seveners (Sabʿiyyah), considered Ismāʿīl the seventh and last of the imams. The majority of Ismāʿīlīs, however, believed that the imamate continued in the line of Ismāʿīl's descendants. The Ismāʿīlī teaching spread during the 9th century from North Africa to Sind, in India, and the Ismāʿīlī Fāṭimid dynasty succeeded in establishing a prosperous empire in Egypt. Ismāʿīlīs are subdivided into two groups—the Nizārīs, headed by the Aga Khan, and the Mustaʿlīs in Mumbai, with their own spiritual head. The Ismāʿīlīs are to be found mainly in East Africa, Pakistan, India, and Yemen.

In their theology, the Ismāʿīlīs have absorbed the most extreme elements and heterodox ideas. The universe is viewed as a cyclic process, and the unfolding of each cycle is marked by the advent of seven "speakers"—messengers of God with scriptures—each of whom is succeeded by seven "silents"—messengers without revealed scriptures; the last speaker (the Prophet Muhammad) is followed by seven imams who interpret the Will of God to humanity and are, in a sense, higher than the Prophet because they draw their knowledge directly from God and not from the Angel of Inspiration. During the 10th century, certain Ismāʿīlī intellectuals formed a secret society called the Brethren of Purity, which issued a philosophical encyclopaedia, *The Epistles of the Brethren of Purity*, aiming at the liquidation of positive religions in favour of a universalist spirituality.

Aga Khan III (1887–1957) took several measures to bring his followers closer to the main body of the Muslims. The Ismāʿīlīs, however, still have not mosques but *jamāʿat khānahs* ("gathering houses"), and their mode of worship bears little resemblance to that of the Muslims generally.

RELATED SECTS

Several other sects arose out of the general Shīʿite movement—e.g., the Nuṣayrīs, the Yazīdīs, and the Druzes—which are sometimes considered as independent from Islam. The Druzes arose in the 11th century out of a cult of deification of the Fāṭimid caliph al-Ḥākim.

During a 19th-century anticlerical movement in Iran, a certain ʿAlī Moḥammad of Shīrāz appeared, declaring himself to be the Bāb ("Gate"; i.e., to God). At that time the climate in Iran was generally favourable to messianic ideas. He was, however, bitterly opposed by the Shīʿite *ulamā* (council of learned men) and was executed in 1850. After his death, his two disciples, Ṣobḥ-e Azal and Bahāʾ Ullāh, broke and went in different directions. Bahāʾ Ullāh eventually declared his religion—stressing a humanitarian pacificism and universalism—to be an independent religion outside Islam. The Bahāʾī faith won a considerable number of converts in North America during the early 20th century.

DRUZE

The Druze (Arabic plural Durūz, singular Darazi) are a small Middle Eastern religious sect characterized by an eclectic system of doctrines and by a cohesion and loyalty among its members (at times politically significant) that have enabled them to maintain for centuries their close-knit identity and distinctive faith. The Druze numbered more than 1,000,000 in the early 21st century and live mostly in Lebanon, with smaller communities in Israel, Syria, Jordan, and abroad. They call themselves *muwaḥḥidūn* ("monotheists").

The Druze faith originated in Egypt as an offshoot of Ismaʿīlī Shīʿism when, during the reign of the sixth Fāṭimid caliph, al-Ḥākim bi-ʿAmr Allāh (ruled 996–1021), some Ismaʿīlī theologians began to organize a movement proclaiming al-Ḥākim a divine figure. Although the idea was probably encouraged by al-Ḥākim himself, it was condemned as heresy by the Fāṭimid religious establishment, which held that al-Ḥākim and his predecessors were divinely appointed but not themselves divine.

(continued on the next page)

(continued from the previous page)

In 1017 the doctrine was publicly preached for the first time, causing riots in Cairo.

Al-Ḥākim disappeared mysteriously in 1021, and the movement was persecuted under his successor, al-Zāhir. The Druze faith gradually died out in Egypt but survived in isolated areas of Syria and Lebanon, where missionaries had established significant communities.

A group of Druzes stand before Mount Hermon at the Lebanon-Syria border in this *c.* 1901 photograph.

Despite the small size of their community, the Druze have figured prominently in Middle Eastern history. During the Crusades, Druze soldiers aided the Ayyūbid and later Mamlūk forces by resisting Crusader advances at the Lebanese coast. The Druze enjoyed considerable autonomy under the Ottoman Empire and often rebelled against it, protected from direct Ottoman control by the mountainous terrain of their homelands. From the 16th to the 19th century, a series of powerful feudal lords dominated Druze political life. In the 20th and 21st centuries the Druze in Lebanon have mostly been represented in national politics by two families, the Jumblatts and the Arslans.

The Druze permit no conversion, either away from or to their religion. Marriage outside the Druze faith is rare and is strongly discouraged. Many Druze religious practices are kept secret, even from the community as a whole. Only an elite of initiates, known as ʿuqqāl ("knowers"), participate fully in their religious services and have access to the secret teachings of the scriptures, *Al-Ḥikmah al-Sharīfah*.

SUFISM

Islamic mysticism, or Sufism, emerged out of early ascetic reactions on the part of certain religiously sensitive personalities against the general worldliness that had overtaken the Muslim community and the purely "externalist" expressions of Islam in law and theology. These persons stressed the Muslim qualities of moral motivation, contrition against overworldliness, and "the state of the heart" as opposed to the legalist formulations of Islam.

THE AḤMADIYYAH

In the latter half of the 19th century in Punjab, India, Mirza Ghulam Ahmad claimed to be an inspired prophet. At first a defender of Islam against Christian missionaries, he then later adopted certain doctrines of

Members of the Mawlawīyah fraternity of Sufis, commonly known as whirling dervishes, perform their ritual prayer (*dhikr*) by spinning on the right foot to the accompaniment of musical instruments.

the Indian Muslim modernist Sayyid Ahmad Khan—namely, that Jesus died a natural death and was not assumed into heaven as the Islamic orthodoxy believed and that jihad "by the sword" had been abrogated and replaced with jihad "of the pen." His aim appears to have been to synthesize all religions under Islam, for he declared himself to be not only the manifestation of the Prophet Muhammad but also the Second Advent of Jesus, as well as Krishna for the Hindus, among other claims. He did not announce, however, any new revelation or new law.

In 1914 a schism over succession occurred among the Ahmadiyyah. One group that seceded from the main body, which was headed by a son of the founder, disowned the prophetic claims of Ghulam Ahmad and established its centre in Lahore (now in Pakistan). The main body of the Ahmadiyyah (known as the Qadiani, after the village of Qadian, birthplace of the founder and the group's first centre) evolved a separatist organization and, after the partition of India in 1947, moved their headquarters to Rabwah in what was then West Pakistan.

Both groups are noted for their missionary work, particularly in the West and in Africa. Within the Muslim countries, however, there is fierce opposition to the main group because of its claim that Ghulam Ahmad was a prophet (most Muslim sects believe in the finality of prophethood with Muhammad) and because of its separatist organization. Restrictions were imposed on the Ahmadiyyah in 1974 and again in 1984 by the Pakistani government, which declared that the group was not Muslim and prohibited them from engaging in various Islamic activities.

CHAPTER 4

ISLAMIC PHILOSOPHY

The origin and inspiration of philosophy in Islam are quite different from those of Islamic theology. Philosophy developed out of the nonreligious practical and theoretical sciences, it recognized no theoretical limits other than those of human reason itself, and it assumed that the truth found by unaided reason does not disagree with the truth of Islam when both are properly understood. Islamic philosophy was not a handmaid of theology. The two disciplines were related, because both engaged in rational inquiry and distinguished themselves from traditional religious disciplines and from mysticism, which sought knowledge through purification. Islamic theology was strictly Islamic: it confined itself within the Islamic religious community, and it remained separate from the Christian and Jewish theologies that developed in the same cultural context and used Arabic as a linguistic medium. No such separation is observable in the philosophy developed in the Islamic cultural context and written in Arabic: Muslims, Christians, and Jews participated in it and separated themselves according to the philosophic rather than the religious doctrines they held.

THE EASTERN PHILOSOPHERS

The background of philosophic interest in Islam is found in the earlier phases of theology. But its origin is found in the translation

65

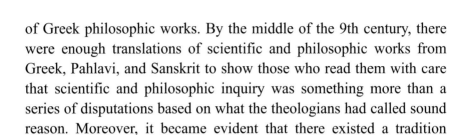

of Greek philosophic works. By the middle of the 9th century, there were enough translations of scientific and philosophic works from Greek, Pahlavi, and Sanskrit to show those who read them with care that scientific and philosophic inquiry was something more than a series of disputations based on what the theologians had called sound reason. Moreover, it became evident that there existed a tradition of observation, calculation, and theoretical reflection that had been pursued systematically, refined, and modified for over a millennium.

The scope of this tradition was broad: it included the study of logic, the sciences of nature (including psychology and biology), the mathematical sciences (including music and astronomy), metaphysics, ethics, and politics. Each of these disciplines had a body of literature in which its principles and problems had been investigated by Classical authors, whose positions had been, in turn, stated, discussed, criticized, or developed by various commentators. Islamic philosophy emerged from its theological background when Muslim thinkers began to study this foreign tradition, became competent students of the ancient philosophers and scientists, criticized and developed their doctrines, clarified their relevance for the questions raised by the theologians, and showed what light they threw on the fundamental issues of revelation, prophecy, and the divine law.

THE TEACHINGS OF AL-KINDĪ

Although the first Muslim philosopher, al-Kindī, who flourished in the first half of the 9th century, lived during the triumph of the Muʿtazilah of Baghdad and was connected with the ʿAbbāsid caliphs who championed the Muʿtazilah and patronized the Hellenistic sciences, there is no clear evidence that he belonged to a theological school. His writings show him to have been a diligent student of Greek and Hellenistic

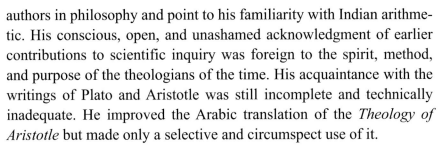

authors in philosophy and point to his familiarity with Indian arithmetic. His conscious, open, and unashamed acknowledgment of earlier contributions to scientific inquiry was foreign to the spirit, method, and purpose of the theologians of the time. His acquaintance with the writings of Plato and Aristotle was still incomplete and technically inadequate. He improved the Arabic translation of the *Theology of Aristotle* but made only a selective and circumspect use of it.

Devoting most of his writings to questions of natural philosophy and mathematics, al-Kindī was particularly concerned with the relation between corporeal things, which are changeable, in constant flux, infinite, and as such unknowable, on the one hand, and the permanent world of forms (spiritual or secondary substances), which are not subject to flux yet to which human beings have no access except through things of the senses. He insisted that a purely human knowledge of all things is possible, through the use of various scientific devices, learning such things as mathematics and logic, and assimilating the contributions of earlier thinkers. The existence of a "supernatural" way to this knowledge in which all these requirements can be dispensed with was acknowledged by al-Kindī: God may choose to impart it to his prophets by cleansing and illuminating their souls and by giving them his aid, right guidance, and inspiration; and they, in turn, communicate it to ordinary human beings in an admirably clear, concise, and comprehensible style. This is the prophets' "divine" knowledge, characterized by a special mode of access and style of exposition. In principle, however, this very same knowledge is accessible to human beings without divine aid, even though "human" knowledge may lack the completeness and consummate logic of the prophets' divine message.

Reflection on the two kinds of knowledge—the human knowledge bequeathed by the ancients and the revealed knowledge expressed in the Qur'ān—led al-Kindī to pose a number of themes

Al-Kindī (flourished 9th century) was the first Muslim philosopher.

that became central to Islamic philosophy: the rational–metaphorical exegesis of the Qurʾān and the Hadith; the identification of God with the first being and the first cause; creation as the giving of being and as a kind of causation distinct from natural causation and Neoplatonic emanation; and the immortality of the individual soul.

THE TEACHINGS OF ABŪ BAKR AL-RĀZĪ

The philosopher whose principal concerns, method, and opposition to authority were inspired by the extreme Muʿtazilah was the physician Abū Bakr al-Rāzī (flourished 9th–10th centuries). He adopted the Muʿtazilah's atomism and was intent on developing a rationally defensible theory of creation that would not require any change in God or attribute to him responsibility for the imperfection and evil prevalent in the created world. To this end, he expounded the view that there are five eternal principles—God, Soul, prime matter, infinite, or absolute, space, and unlimited, or absolute, time—and explained creation as the result of the unexpected and sudden turn of events (*faltah*). Faltah occurred when Soul, in her ignorance, desired matter and the good God eased her misery by allowing her to satisfy her desire and to experience the suffering of the material world, and then gave her reason to make her realize her mistake and deliver her from her union with matter, the cause of her suffering and of all evil. Al-Rāzī claimed that he was a Platonist, that he disagreed with Aristotle, and that his views were those of the Ṣābians of Harran and the Brahmans (the Hindu priestly caste).

Ismāʿīlī theologians became aware of the kinship between certain elements of his cosmology and their own. They disputed with him during his lifetime and continued afterward to refute his doctrines in their writings. According to their account of his doctrines, he was

Al-Rāzī (flourished 9th–10th centuries) is illustrated examining a young patient. In addition to his philosophy, al-Rāzī is recognized as the greatest physician of the Islamic world.

totally opposed to authority in matters of knowledge, believed in the progress of the arts and sciences, and held that all reasonable human beings are equally able to look after their own affairs, equally inspired and able to know the truth of what earlier teachers had taught, and equally able to improve upon it. Ismāʿīlī theologians were incensed, in particular, by his wholesale rejection of prophecy, particular revelation, and divine laws. They were likewise opposed to his criticisms of religion in general as a device employed by evildoers and a kind of tyranny over human beings that exploits their innocence and credulity, perpetuates ignorance, and leads to conflicts and wars.

Although the fragmentary character of al-Kindī's and al-Rāzī's surviving philosophic writings does not permit passing firm and independent judgment on their accomplishments, they tend to bear out the view of later Muslim students of philosophy that both lacked competence in the logical foundation of philosophy, were knowledgeable in some of the natural sciences but not in metaphysics, and were unable to narrow the gap that separated philosophy from the new religion, Islam.

POLITICAL PHILOSOPHY AND THE STUDY OF RELIGION

The first philosopher to meet this challenge was al-Fārābī (flourished 9th–10th centuries). He saw that theology and the juridical study of the law were derivative phenomena that function within a framework set by the prophet as lawgiver and founder of a human community. In this community, revelation defines the opinions the members of the community must hold and the actions they must perform if they are to attain the earthly happiness of this world and the supreme happiness of the other world. Philosophy could not understand this framework of religion as long as it concerned itself almost exclusively with its truth content and confined the study of practical science to individualistic ethics and personal salvation.

In contrast to al-Kindī and al-Rāzī, al-Fārābī recast philosophy in a new framework analogous to that of the Islamic religion. The sciences were organized within this framework so that logic, physics, mathematics, and metaphysics culminated in a political science whose subject matter was the investigation of happiness and how it can be realized in societies. The central theme of this political science is the founder of a virtuous community. Included in this theme are views concerning the supreme rulers who follow the founder, their qualifications, and how the community must be ordered so that its members attain happiness as citizens rather than isolated human beings. Once this new philosophical framework was established, it became possible to conduct a philosophical investigation of the elements that constituted the Islamic community: the prophet-lawgiver, the aims of the divine laws, the legislation of beliefs as well as actions, the role of the successors to the founding legislator, the grounds of the interpretation or reform of the law, the classification of human communities according to their doctrines and size, and the critique of "ignorant" (pagan), "transgressing," "falsifying," and "erring" communities. Al-Fārābī blended philosophical

Al-Fārābī (flourished 9th–10th centuries) was regarded in the medieval Islamic world as the greatest philosophical authority after Aristotle. His portrait appears on the Kazakhstani one-tenge bill.

cosmology, psychology, and politics into a political theology whose aim was to clarify the foundations of the Islamic community and defend its reform in a direction that would promote scientific inquiry and encourage philosophers to play an active role in practical affairs.

INTERPRETATION OF PLATO AND ARISTOTLE

Behind this public aspect of al-Fārābī's work stood a massive body of more properly philosophic or scientific inquiries, which established his reputation among Muslims as the greatest philosophical authority after Aristotle, a great interpreter of Platonic and Aristotelian thought, and a master to whom almost all major Muslim as well as a number of Jewish and Christian philosophers turned for a fuller understanding of the controversial and troublesome questions of philosophy. Continuing the tradition of the Hellenistic masters of the Athenian and Alexandrian philosophical schools, al-Fārābī broadened the range of philosophical inquiry and fixed its form. He paid special attention to the study of language and its relation to logic. In his numerous commentaries on Aristotle's logical works, he expounded for the first time in Arabic the entire range of the scientific and nonscientific forms of argument and established the place of logic as an indispensable prerequisite for philosophic inquiry. His writings on natural science exposed the foundation and assumptions of Aristotle's physics and dealt with the arguments of Aristotle's opponents, both philosophers and scientists, pagan, Christian, and Muslim.

THE ANALOGY OF RELIGION AND PHILOSOPHY

Al-Fārābī's theological and political writings showed later Muslim philosophers the way to deal with the question of the relation between philosophy and religion and presented them with a complex set of problems that they continued to elaborate, modify, and develop in different directions. Starting with the view that religion is analogous or similar to philosophy, al-Fārābī argued that the idea of the true prophet-lawgiver ought to be the same as that of the true philosopher-king. Thus, he challenged both al-Kindī's view that prophets and philosophers have different and independent ways to the highest truth available to human beings and al-Rāzī's view that philosophy is the only way to that knowledge. That a person could combine the functions of prophecy, lawgiving, philosophy, and kingship did not necessarily mean that these functions were identical; it did mean, however, that they all are legitimate subjects of philosophic inquiry. Philosophy must account for the powers, knowledge, and activities of the prophet, lawgiver, and king, which it must distinguish from and relate to those of the philosopher. The public, or political, function of philosophy was emphasized. Unlike Neoplatonism, which had for long limited itself to the Platonic teaching that the function of philosophy is to liberate the soul from the shadowy existence of the cave—in which knowledge can only be imperfectly comprehended as shadows reflecting the light of the truth beyond the cave (the world of senses)—al-Fārābī insisted with Plato that the philosopher must be forced to return to the cave, learn to talk to its inhabitants in a manner they can comprehend, and engage in actions that may improve their lot.

IMPACT ON ISMĀʿĪLĪ THEOLOGY

Although it is not always easy to know the immediate practical intentions of a philosopher, it must be remembered that in al-Fārābī's lifetime the fate of the Islamic world was in the balance. The Sunni caliphate's power hardly extended beyond Baghdad, and it appeared

quite likely that the various Shī'ite sects, especially the Ismāʿīlīs, would finally overpower it and establish a new political order. Of all the movements in Islamic theology, Ismāʿīlī theology was the one that was most clearly and massively penetrated by philosophy. Yet, its Neoplatonic cosmology, revolutionary background, antinomianism (antilegalism), and general expectation that divine laws were about to become superfluous with the appearance of the *qāʾim* (the imam of the "resurrection") all militated against the development of a coherent political theory to meet the practical demands of political life and present a viable practical alternative to the Sunni caliphate. Al-Fārābī's theologico-political writings helped point out this basic defect of Ismāʿīlī theology. Under the Fāṭimids in Egypt (969–1171), Ismāʿīlī theology modified its cosmology in the direction suggested by al-Fārābī, returned to the view that the community must continue to live under the divine law, and postponed the prospect of the abolition of divine laws and the appearance of the *qāʾim* to an indefinite point in the future.

THE "ORIENTAL PHILOSOPHY"

Even more indicative of al-Fārābī's success is the fact that his writings helped produce a philosopher of the stature of Avicenna (flourished 10th–11th centuries), whose versatility, imagination, inventiveness, and prudence shaped philosophy into a powerful force that gradually penetrated Islamic theology and mysticism and Persian poetry in Eastern Islam and gave them universality and theoretical depth. His own personal philosophic views, he said, were those of the ancient sages of Greece (including the genuine views of Plato and Aristotle), which he had set forth in the *Oriental Philosophy*, a book that has not survived and probably was not written or meant to be written. They

were not identical with the common Peripatetic (Aristotelian) doctrines and were to be distinguished from the learning of his contemporaries, the Christian "Aristotelians" of Baghdad, which he attacked as vulgar, distorted, and falsified. His most voluminous writing, *Kitāb al-shifā'* ("The Book of Healing"), was meant to accommodate the doctrines of other philosophers as well as hint at his own personal views, which are elaborated elsewhere in more imaginative and allegorical forms.

Avicenna (flourished 10th–11th centuries) in a woodcut illustration from *Liber chronicarum* ("The Nuremberg Chronicle"), published in 1493.

Distinction between Essence and Existence and the Doctrine of Creation

Avicenna had learned from certain hints in al-Fārābī that the exoteric teachings of Plato regarding the forms, creation, and the immortality of individual souls were closer to revealed doctrines than the genuine views of Aristotle, that the doctrines of Plotinus and later Neoplatonic commentators were useful in harmonizing Aristotle's views with revealed doctrines, and that philosophy must accommodate itself to the divine law on the issue of creation and of reward and punishment in the hereafter, which presupposes some form of individual immortality. Following al-Fārābī's lead, Avicenna initiated a full-fledged inquiry into the question of being, in which he distinguished between essence and existence. He argued that the fact of existence cannot be inferred from or accounted for by the essence of existing things and that form and matter by themselves cannot interact and originate the movement of the universe or the progressive actualization of existing things. Existence must, therefore, be due to an agent-cause that necessitates, imparts, gives, or adds existence to an essence. To do so, the cause must be an existing thing and coexist with its effect. The universe consists of a chain of actual beings, each giving existence to the one below it and responsible for the existence of the rest of the chain below. Because an actual infinite is deemed impossible by Avicenna, this chain as a whole must terminate in a being that is wholly simple and one, whose essence is its very existence, and therefore is self-sufficient and not in need of something else to give it existence. Because its existence is not contingent on or necessitated by something else but is necessary and eternal in itself, it satisfies the condition of being the necessitating cause of the entire chain that constitutes the eternal world of contingent existing things.

All creation is necessarily and eternally dependent upon God. It consists of the intelligences, souls, and bodies of the heavenly spheres, each of which is eternal, and the sublunary sphere, which is also eternal, undergoing a perpetual process of generation and corruption, of the succession of form over matter, in the manner described by Aristotle.

THE IMMORTALITY OF INDIVIDUAL SOULS

There is, however, a significant exception to this general rule: the human rational soul. One can affirm the existence of one's soul from direct consciousness of one's self (what one means by "I"), and one can imagine this happening even in the absence of external objects and bodily organs. This proves, according to Avicenna, that the soul is indivisible, immaterial, and incorruptible substance, not imprinted in matter, but created with the body, which it uses as an instrument. Unlike other immaterial substances (the intelligences and souls of the spheres), it is not pre-eternal but is generated, or made to exist, at the same time as the individual body, which can receive it, is formed. The composition, shape, and disposition of its body and the soul's success or failure in managing and controlling it, the formation of moral habits, and the acquisition of knowledge all contribute to its individuality and difference from other souls. Though the body is not resurrected after its corruption, the soul survives and retains all the individual characteristics, perfections or imperfections, that it achieved in its earthly existence and in this sense is rewarded or punished for its past deeds. Avicenna's claim that he has presented a philosophic proof for the immortality of generated ("created") individual souls no doubt constitutes the high point of his effort to harmonize philosophy and religious beliefs.

Philosophy, Religion, and Mysticism

Having accounted for the more difficult issues of creation and the immortality of individual souls, Avicenna proceeded to explain the faculty of prophetic knowledge (the "sacred" intellect), revelation (imaginative representation meant to convince the multitude and improve their earthly life), miracles, and the legal and institutional arrangements (acts of worship and the regulation of personal and public life) through which the divine law achieves its end. Avicenna's explanation of almost every aspect of Islam is pursued on the basis of extensive exegesis of the Qur'ān and the Hadith. The primary function of religion is to assure the happiness of the many. This practical aim of religion (which Avicenna saw in the perspective of Aristotle's practical science) enabled him to appreciate the political and moral functions of divine revelation and account for its form and content. Revealed religion, however, has a subsidiary function also—that of indicating to the few the need to pursue the kind of life and knowledge appropriate to rare individuals endowed with special gifts. These individuals must be dominated by the love of God to facilitate the achievement of the highest knowledge. In many places Avicenna appears to identify these individuals with the mystics. The identification of the philosopher as a kind of mystic conveyed a new image of the philosopher as a member of the religious community who is distinguished from his coreligionists by his otherworldliness, dedicated to the inner truth of religion, and consumed by the love of God.

Avicenna's allegorical and mystical writings are usually called "esoteric" in the sense that they contain his personal views cast in an imaginative, symbolic form. The esoteric works must, then, be interpreted. Their interpretation must move away from the explicit doctrines contained in "exoteric" works such as the *Shifā'* and recover "the unmixed and uncorrupted truth" set forth in the *Oriental Philosophy*—the existence of which, as noted above, is spurious. This dilemma has made interpretation both difficult and rewarding for Muslim philosophers and modern scholars alike.

THE WESTERN PHILOSOPHERS

Andalusia (in Spain) and western North Africa contributed little of substance to Islamic theology and philosophy until the 12th century. Legal strictures against the study of philosophy were more effective there than in the East. Scientific interest was channelled into medicine, pharmacology, mathematics, astronomy, and logic. More general questions of physics and metaphysics were treated sparingly and in symbols, hints, and allegories. By the 12th century, however, the writings of al-Fārābī, Avicenna, and al-Ghazālī had found their way to the West. A philosophical tradition emerged, based primarily on the study of al-Fārābī. It was critical of Avicenna's philosophic innovations and not convinced that al-Ghazālī's critique of Avicenna touched philosophy as such, and it refused to acknowledge the position assigned by both to mysticism. The survival of philosophy in the West required extreme prudence, emphasis on its scientific character, abstention from meddling in political or religious matters, and abandonment of the hope of effecting extensive doctrinal or institutional reform.

Theoretical Science and Intuitive Knowledge

Ibn Bājjah (died 1138) initiated this tradition with a radical interpretation of al-Fārābī's political philosophy that emphasized the virtues of the perfect but nonexistent city and the vices prevalent in all existing cities. He concluded that the philosopher must order his own life as a solitary individual, shun the company of nonphilosophers, reject their opinions and ways of life, and concentrate on reaching his own final goal by pursuing the theoretical sciences and achieving intuitive knowledge through contact with the Active Intelligence. The multitude live in a dark cave and see only dim shadows. Their ways of life and their imaginings and beliefs consist of layers of darkness that cannot be known through reason alone. Therefore, the divine law has been revealed to enable human beings to know this dark region. The philosopher's duty is to seek the light of the sun (the intellect). To do so, he must leave the cave, see all colours as they truly are and see light itself, and finally become transformed into that light. The end, then, is contact with

Intelligence, not with something that transcends Intelligence, as taught by Plotinus, Ismāʿīlism, and mysticism. Ibn Bājjah criticized the latter as the way of imagination, motivated by desire, and aiming at pleasure. Philosophy, he claimed, is the only way to the truly blessed state, which can be achieved only by going through theoretical science, even though it is higher than theoretical science.

UNCONCERN OF PHILOSOPHY WITH REFORM

Ibn Bājjah's cryptic style and the unfinished form in which he left most of his writings tend to highlight his departures

Ibn Bājjah (died 1138) was the earliest known representative in Spain of the Arabic Aristotelian-Neoplatonic philosophical tradition.

from al-Fārābī and Avicenna. Unlike al-Fārābī, he is silent about the philosopher's duty to return to the cave and partake of the life of the city. He appears to argue that the aim of philosophy is attainable independently from the philosopher's concern with the best city and is to be achieved in solitude or, at most, in comradeship with philosophic souls. Unlike Avicenna, who prepared the way for him by clearly distinguishing between theoretical and practical science, Ibn Bājjah is concerned with practical science only insofar as it is relevant to the life of the philosopher. He is contemptuous of allegories and imaginative

representations of philosophic knowledge, silent about theology, and shows no concern with improving the multitude's way of life.

THE PHILOSOPHER AS A SOLITARY INDIVIDUAL

In his philosophic story *Ḥayy ibn Yaqẓān* ("Alive, Son of Wakeful"), the philosopher Ibn Ṭufayl (died 1185) fills gaps in the work of his predecessor Ibn Bājjah. The story communicates the secrets of Avicenna's *Oriental Philosophy* as experienced by a solitary hero who grows up on a deserted island, learns about the things around him, acquires knowledge of the natural universe (including the heavenly bodies), and achieves the state of "annihilation" (*fanā'*) of the self in the divine reality. This is the apparent and traditional secret of the *Oriental Philosophy.* But the hero's wisdom is still incomplete, for he knows nothing about other human beings, their way of life, or their laws. When he chances to meet one of them—a member of a religious community inhabiting a neighbouring island, who is inclined to reflect on the divine law and seek its inner, spiritual meanings and who has abandoned the society of his fellow human beings to devote himself to solitary meditation and worship—he does not at first recognize that he is a human being like himself, cannot communicate with him, and frightens him by his wild aspect. After learning about the doctrines and acts of worship of the religious community, he understands them as alluding to and agreeing with the truth that he had learned by his own unaided effort, and he goes as far as admitting the validity of the religion and the truthfulness of the prophet who gave it. He cannot understand, however, why the Prophet Muhammad communicated the truth by way of allusions, examples, and corporeal representations or why religion permits human beings to devote much time and effort to practical, worldly things.

CONCERN FOR REFORM

His ignorance of the nature of most people and his compassion for them make the solitary hero insist on becoming their saviour. He persuades his companion to take him to his coreligionists and help him convert them to the naked truth by propagating among them "the secrets of wisdom." His education is completed when he fails in his endeavour. He learns the limits beyond which the multitude cannot ascend without becoming confused and unhappy. He also learns the wisdom of the divine lawgiver in addressing them in the way they can understand, enabling them to achieve limited ends through doctrines and actions suited to their abilities. The story ends with the hero taking leave of these people after apologizing to them for what he did and confessing that he is now fully convinced that they should not change their ways but remain attached to the literal sense of the divine law and obey its demands. He returns to his own island to continue his former solitary existence.

THE HIDDEN SECRET OF AVICENNA'S "ORIENTAL PHILOSOPHY"

The hidden secret of Avicenna's *Oriental Philosophy* appears, then, to be that the philosopher must return to the cave, educate himself in the ways of nonphilosophers, and understand the incompatibility between philosophical life and the life of the multitude, which must be governed by religion and divine laws. Otherwise, his ignorance will lead him to actions dangerous to the well-being of both the community and philosophy. Because Ibn Ṭufayl's hero had grown up as a solitary human being, he lacks the kind of wisdom that could have enabled him

83

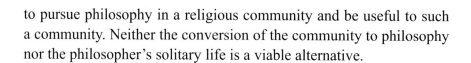

to pursue philosophy in a religious community and be useful to such a community. Neither the conversion of the community to philosophy nor the philosopher's solitary life is a viable alternative.

PHILOSOPHY

To Ibn Ṭufayl's younger friend Averroës (Ibn Rushd, flourished 12th century) belongs the distinction of presenting a solution to the problem of the relation between philosophy and the Islamic community in the West, a solution meant to be legally valid, theologically sound, and philosophically satisfactory. Here was a philosopher fully at home in what Ibn Bājjah had called the many layers of darkness. His legal training (he was a judge by profession) and his extensive knowledge of the history of the religious sciences (including theology) enabled him to speak with authority about the principles of Islamic law and their application to theological and philosophic issues and to question the authority of al-Ghazālī and the Ashʿarīs to determine correct beliefs and right practices. He was able to examine in detail from the point of view of the divine law the respective claims of theology and philosophy to possess the best and surest way to human knowledge, to be competent to interpret the ambiguous expressions of the divine law, and to have presented convincing arguments that are theoretically tenable and practically salutary.

THE DIVINE LAW

The intention of the divine law, he argued, is to assure the happiness of all members of the community. This requires everyone to profess belief in the basic principles of religion as enunciated in the Qurʾān,

84

the Hadith, and the *ijmā'* (consensus) of the learned and to perform all obligatory acts of worship. Beyond this, the only just requirement is to demand that each pursue knowledge as far as his natural capacity and makeup permit. The few who are endowed with the capacity for the highest, demonstrative knowledge are under a divine legal obligation to pursue the highest wisdom, which is philosophy, and they need not constantly adjust its certain conclusions to what theologians claim to be the correct interpretation of the divine law. Being dialecticians and rhetoricians, theologians are not in a position to determine what is and is not correct interpretation of the divine law so far as philosophers are concerned. The divine law directly authorizes philosophers to pursue its interpretation according to the best—i.e., demonstrative

Averröes (flourished 12th century; *right*) is depicted in a detail from *The Triumph of St. Thomas Aquinas* by the renowned 14th-century Florentine painter Andrea da Firenze.

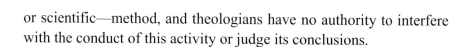

or scientific—method, and theologians have no authority to interfere with the conduct of this activity or judge its conclusions.

THEOLOGY

On the basis of this legal doctrine, Averroës judged the theologian al-Ghazālī's refutation of the philosophers ineffective and inappropriate because al-Ghazālī did not understand and even misrepresented the philosophers' positions and used arguments that only demonstrate his incompetence in the art of demonstration. He criticized al-Fārābī and Avicenna also for accommodating the theologians of their time and for departing from the path of the ancient philosophers merely to please the theologians. At the other extreme are the multitude for whom there are no more convincing arguments than those found in the divine law itself. Neither philosophers nor theologians are permitted to disclose to the multitude interpretations of the ambiguous verses of the Qur'ān or to confuse them with their own doubts or arguments. Finally, there are those who belong to neither the philosophers nor the multitude, either because they are naturally superior to the multitude but not endowed with the gift for philosophy or because they are students in initial stages of philosophic training. For this intermediate group, theology is necessary. It is an intermediate discipline that is neither strictly legal nor philosophic. It lacks their certain principles and sure methods. Therefore, theology must remain under the constant control of philosophy and the supervision of the divine law so as not to drift into taking positions that cannot be demonstrated philosophically or that are contrary to the intention of the divine law. Averroës himself composed a work on theology, *Kitāb al-kashf ʿan manāhij al-adillah* ("Exposition of the Methods of Proofs"), to show how these requirements can be met. In the Latin West he was best known for his philosophical answer

to al-Ghazālī, *Tahāfut al-tahāfut* ("Incoherence of the Incoherence"), and for his extensive commentaries on Aristotle, works that left their impact on medieval and Renaissance European thought.

THE NEW WISDOM: SYNTHESIS OF PHILOSOPHY AND MYSTICISM

The Western tradition in Islamic philosophy formed part of the Arabic philosophic literature that was translated into Hebrew and Latin and that played a significant role in the development of medieval philosophy in the Latin West and the emergence of modern European philosophy. Its impact on the development of philosophy in Eastern Islam was not as dramatic but was important nevertheless. Students of this tradition— e.g., the prominent Jewish philosopher Maimonides (flourished 12th century) and the historian Ibn Khaldūn (flourished 14th century)— moved to Egypt, where they taught and had numerous disciples. Most of the writings of Ibn Bājjah, Ibn Ṭufayl, and Averroës found their way to the East also, where they were studied alongside the writings of their Eastern predecessors. In both regions thinkers who held to the idea of philosophy as formulated by the Eastern and Western philosophers thus far discussed continued to teach. They became isolated and overwhelmed, however, by the resurgence of traditionalism and the emergence of a new kind of philosophy whose champions looked on the earlier masters as men who had made significant contributions to the progress of knowledge but whose overall view was defective and had now become outdated.

Resurgent traditionalism found effective defenders in men such as Ibn Taymiyyah (13th–14th centuries), who employed a massive battery of philosophic, theological, and legal arguments against every shade of innovation and called for a return to the beliefs and practices

87

The movement of Western medieval philosophers—
such as the Jewish philosopher Maimonides, who
studied Western Islamic philosophers before
moving east to Egypt in the 1160s—helped bring the
Western tradition of Islamic philosophy east.

of the pious ancestors. These attacks, however, did not deal a decisive blow to philosophy as such. It rather drove philosophy underground for a period, only to re-emerge in a new garb. A more important reason for the decline of the earlier philosophic tradition, however, was the renewed vitality and success of the program formulated by al-Ghazālī for the integration of theology, philosophy, and mysticism into a new kind of philosophy called wisdom (*hikmah*). It consisted of a critical review of the philosophy of Avicenna, preserving its main external features (its logical, physical, and, in part, metaphysical structure, and its terminology) and introducing principles of explanation for the universe and its relation to God based on personal experience and direct vision.

CHARACTERISTIC FEATURES OF THE NEW WISDOM

If the popular theology preached by the philosophers from al-Fārābī to Averroës is disregarded, it is evident that philosophy proper meant to them what al-Fārābī called a state of mind dedicated to the quest and the love for the highest wisdom. None of them claimed, however, that he had achieved this highest wisdom. In contrast, every leading exponent of the new wisdom stated that he had achieved or received it through a private illumination, dream (at times inspired by the Prophet Muhammad), or vision and on this basis proceeded to give an explanation of the inner structure of natural and divine things. In every case, this explanation incorporated Platonic or Aristotelian elements but was more akin to some version of a later Hellenistic philosophy, which had found its way earlier into one or another of the schools of Islamic theology, though, because of the absence of an adequate philosophic education on the part of earlier theologians, it had not been either elaborated or integrated into a comprehensive view. Like their late Hellenistic counterparts, exponents of the new wisdom proceeded through an examination of the positions of Plato, Aristotle, and Plotinus. They also gave special attention to the insights of the pre-Socratic philosophers of ancient Greece and the myths and revelations of the ancient Middle East, and they offered to resolve the fundamental questions that had puzzled earlier philosophers. In its basic movement and general direction, therefore, Islamic philosophy between the 9th and 19th centuries followed a course parallel to that of Greek philosophy from the 5th century BCE to the 6th century CE.

PRIMARY TEACHERS OF THE NEW WISDOM

Several prominent Islamic thinkers developed the so-called new wisdom, expounding upon its blend of Aristotelianism and Neoplatonism with Islamic theology.

THE TEACHINGS OF AL-SUHRAWARDĪ

The first master of the new wisdom, al-Suhrawardī (12th century), called it the "wisdom of illumination." He rejected Avicenna's distinction between essence and existence and Aristotle's distinction between substance and accidents, possibility and actuality, and matter and form on the ground that they are mere distinctions of reason. Instead, he concentrated on the notion of being and its negation, which he called "light" and "darkness," and explained the gradation of beings

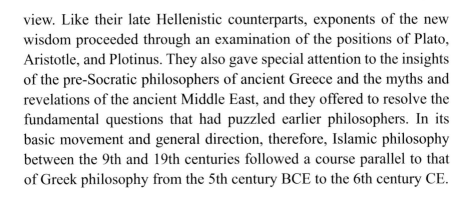

CRITIQUES OF ARISTOTLE

The critiques of Aristotle that began in Muʿtazilī circles and found a prominent champion in Abū Bakr al-Rāzī were provided

with a more solid foundation in the 10th and 11th centuries by th Christian theologians and philosophers of Baghdad. The latte translated the writings of the Hellenistic critics of Aristotle, such a John Philoponus, and made use of their arguments in commenting on Aristotle and in independent theological and philosophic works. Avicenna's attack on these so-called Aristotelians and their Hellenistic predecessors (an attack that had been initiated by al-Fārābī and was to be continued by Averroës) did not prevent the spread of their theologically based anti-Aristotelianism among Jewish and Muslim students of philosophy in the 12th century such as Abū al-Barakāt al-Baghdādī (died c. 1175) and Fakh al-Dīn al-Rāzī. These theologians continued and intensified al-Ghazālī's attacks on Avicenna and Aristotle (especially thei views on time, movement, matter, and form, the nature of the heavenly bodies, and the relation between the intelligible and sensible worlds). They suggested that a thorough examination of Aristotle had revealed to them, on philosophic grounds, that the fundamental disagreements between him and the theologies based on the revealed religions represented open options and that Aristotle's view of the universe was in need of explanatory principles that could very well be supplied by theology. This critique

Muslim thinkers in the 10th–12th centuries greatly debated whether or not the shortcomings of Aristotle's worldview could be resolved by Islamic theology. These debates laid the groundwork for later philosophers to attempt to reconcile philosophy and theology.

(continued on the next page)

(continued from the previous page)

provided the framework for the integration of philosophy into theology from the 13th century onward.

Although it made use of such theological criticisms of philosophy, the new wisdom took the position that theology did not offer a positive substitute for and was incapable of solving the difficulties of "Aristotelian" philosophy. It did not question the need to have recourse to the Qur'ān and the Hadith to find the right answers. It insisted (on the authority of a long-standing mystical tradition), however, that theology concerns itself only with the external expressions of this divine source of knowledge. The inner core was reserved for the adepts of the mystic path whose journey leads to the experience of the highest reality in dreams and visions. Only the mystical adepts are in possession of the one true wisdom, the ground of both the external expressions of the divine law and the phenomenal world of human experience and thought.

as gradation of their mixture according to the degree of "strength," or "perfection," of their light. This gradation forms a single continuum that culminates in pure light, self-luminosity, self-awareness, self-manifestation, or self-knowledge, which is God, the light of lights, the true One. The stability and eternity of this single continuum result from every higher light overpowering and subjugating the lower, and movement and change in it result from each of the lower lights desiring and loving the higher.

Al-Suhrawardī's "pan-lightism" is not particularly close to traditional Islamic views concerning the creation of the world and God's knowledge of particulars. The structure of his universe remains largely that of the Platonists and the Aristotelians. And his account of the emanation process avoids the many difficulties that had puzzled Neoplatonists as they tried to understand how the second hypostasis

(reality) proceeds from the One. He asserted that it proceeds without in any way affecting the One and that the One's self-sufficiency is enough to explain the giving out that seems to be both spontaneous and necessary. His doctrine is presented in a way that suggests that it is the inner truth behind the exoteric (external) teachings of Islam as well as Zoroastrianism, indeed the wisdom of all ancient sages, especially Iranians and Greeks, and the revealed religions as well. This neutral yet positive attitude toward the diversity of religions, which was not absent among Muslim philosophers and mystics, was to become one of the hallmarks of the new wisdom. Different religions were seen as different manifestations of the same truth, their essential agreement was emphasized, and various attempts were made to combine them into a single harmonious religion meant for all humankind.

Al-Suhrawardī takes an important step in this direction through his doctrine of imaginative-bodily "resurrection." After their departure from the prison of the body, souls that are fully purified ascend directly to the world of separate lights. The ones that are only partially purified or are evil souls escape to a "world of images" suspended below the higher lights and above the corporeal world. In this world of images, or forms (not to be confused with the Platonic forms, which al-Suhrawardī identifies with higher and permanent intelligible lights), partially purified souls remain suspended and are able to create for themselves and by their own power of imagination pleasing figures and desirable objects in forms more excellent than their earthly counterparts and are able to enjoy them forever. Evil souls become dark shadows, suffer (presumably because their corrupt and inefficient power of imagination can create only ugly and frightening forms), and wander about as ghosts, demons, and devils. The creative power of the imagination, which as a human psychological phenomenon was already used by the philosophers to explain prophetic powers, was seized upon by the new wisdom as "divine magic." It was used to construct an

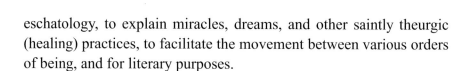

eschatology, to explain miracles, dreams, and other saintly theurgic (healing) practices, to facilitate the movement between various orders of being, and for literary purposes.

THE TEACHINGS OF IBN AL-ʿARABĪ

The account of the doctrines of Ibn al-ʿArabī (12th–13th centuries) belongs properly to the history of Islamic mysticism. Yet his impact on the subsequent development of the new wisdom was in many ways far greater than was that of al-Suhrawardī. This is true especially of his central doctrine of the "unity of being" and his sharp distinction between the absolute One, which is undefinable Truth (*ḥaqq*), and his self-manifestation (*ẓuhūr*), or creation (*khalq*), which is ever new (*jadīd*) and in perpetual movement, a movement that unites the whole of creation in a process of constant renewal. At the very core of this dynamic edifice stands nature, the "dark cloud" (*ʿamāʾ*) or "mist" (*bukhār*), as the ultimate principle of things and forms: intelligence, heavenly bodies, and elements and their mixtures that culminate in the "perfect man." This primordial nature is the "breath" of the Merciful God in his aspect as Lord. It "flows" throughout the universe and manifests Truth in all its parts. It is the first mother through which Truth manifests itself to itself and generates the universe. And it is the universal natural body that gives birth to the translucent bodies of the spheres, to the elements, and to their mixtures, all of which are related to that primary source as daughters to their mother.

Ibn al-ʿArabī attempted to explain how Intelligence proceeds from the absolute One by inserting between them a primordial feminine principle, which is all things in potentiality but which also possesses the capacity, readiness, and desire to manifest or generate them first as archetypes in Intelligence and then as actually existing things in the universe below. Ibn al-ʿArabī gave this principle numerous names, including prime "matter" (*unṣur*), and characterized it as the principle "whose existence makes manifest the essences of the potential worlds." The doctrine that the first simple originated thing is not Intelligence but "indefinite matter" and that Intelligence was originated through the mediation of this matter was attributed to Empedocles, a 5th-century-BCE Greek philosopher, in doxographies (compilations of extracts from the Greek philosophers) translated into Arabic. It represented an attempt to bridge the gulf between the absolute One and the multiplicity of forms in Intelligence. The Andalusian mystic Ibn Masarrah (9th–10th centuries) is reported to have championed pseudo-Empedoclean doctrines, and Ibn al-ʿArabī (who studied under some of his followers) quotes Ibn Masarrah on a number of occasions. This philosophic tradition is distinct from the one followed by the Ismāʿīlī theologians, who explained the origination of Intelligence by the mediation of God's will.

THE TEACHINGS OF TWELVER SHĪʿISM AND THE SCHOOL OF EṢFAHĀN

After Ibn al-ʿArabī, the new wisdom developed rapidly in intellectual circles in Eastern Islam. Commentators on the works of Avicenna, al-Suhrawardī, and Ibn al-ʿArabī began the process of harmonizing and integrating the views of the masters. Great poets made them part of every educated person's literary culture. Mystical fraternities became the custodians of such works, spreading them into Central Asia and the Indian subcontinent and transmitting them from one generation to another. Following the Mongol khan Hülagü's entry into Baghdad (1258), the Twelver Shīʿites were encouraged by the Il Khanid Tatars and Naṣīr al-Dīn al-Ṭūsī (the philosopher and theologian who accompanied Hülagü as his vizier) to abandon their hostility to mysticism. Muʿtazilī doctrines were retained in their theology. Theology, however, was downgraded to "formal" learning that must be supplemented by higher things, the latter including philosophy and mysticism, both of earlier Shīʿite (including Ismāʿīlī) origin and of later Sunni provenance. Al-Ghazālī, al-Suhrawardī, Ibn al-ʿArabī, and Avicenna were then eagerly studied and (except for their doctrine of the imamate) embraced with little or no reservation. This movement in Shīʿite thought gathered momentum when the leaders of a mystical fraternity established themselves as the Ṣafavid dynasty (1501–1732) in Iran, where they championed Twelver Shīʿism as the official doctrine of the new monarchy. During the 17th century, Iran experienced a cultural and scientific renaissance that included a revival of philosophic studies. There, Islamic philosophy found its last creative exponents. The new wisdom as expounded by the masters of the school of Eṣfahān radiated throughout Eastern Islam and continued as a vital tradition until modern times.

The major figures of the school of Eṣfahān were Mīr Dāmād (Muḥammad Bāqir ibn al-Dāmād, died 1631/32) and his great disciple Mullā Ṣadrā (Ṣadr al-Dīn al-Shīrāzī, c. 1571–1640). Both were men of wide culture and prolific writers with a sharp sense for the history and development of philosophic ideas.

The Teachings of Mīr Dāmād

Mīr Dāmād was the first to expound the notion of "eternal origination" (ḥudūth dahrī) as an explanation for the creation of the world. Muslim philosophers and their critics had recognized the crucial role played by the question of time in the discussion of the eternity of the world. The proposition that time is the measure of movement was criticized by Abū al-Barakāt al-Baghdādī, who argued that time is prior to movement and rest, indeed to everything except being. Time is the measure or concomitant of being, lasting and transient, enduring and in movement or rest. It characterizes or qualifies all being, including God. God

The 17th-century Masjed-e Emām (Persian: "Imam Mosque") in Eṣfahān, Iran, is representative of Ṣafavid architecture. Twelver Shīʿism was the official doctrine of the Ṣafavid dynasty.

works in time, incessantly willing and directly creating everything in the world: his persistent will creates the eternal beings of the world, and his ever-renewed will creates the transient beings. The notion of a God who works in time was of course objectionable to theology, and Fakhr al-Dīn al-Rāzī refused to accept this solution despite its attractions. Al-Rāzī also saw that it leads to the notion (attributed to Plato) that time is a self-subsistent substance, whose relation to God would further compromise his unity. Finally, al-Rāzī explained that this self-subsistent substance will have to be related to different beings in different ways. It is called "everlastingness" (*sarmad*) when related to God and the Intelligences (angels) that are permanent and do not move or change in any way, "eternity" (*dahr*) when related to the totality of the world of movement and change, and "time" (*zamān*) when related to corporeal beings that make up the world of movement and change.

Mīr Dāmād returned to Avicenna and sought to harmonize his views with those of al-Suhrawardī on the assumption that what Avicenna meant by his "Oriental" (*mashriqiyyah*) philosophy was identical with al-Suhrawardī's wisdom of "illumination" (*ishrāq*), which he interpreted as a Platonic doctrine that asserted the priority of essence (form) over being (existence). Time, for Mīr Dāmād, was neither a mere being of reason nor an accident of existing things. It belongs to the essence of things and describes their mode and rank of being. It is a "relation" that beings have to each other because of their essential nature. There must, therefore, be three ranks of order of time corresponding to the three ranks of order of being. Considered as the relation of God to the divine names and attributes (Intelligences or archetypes), the relation is "everlastingness." Considered as the relation between the Intelligences, or archetypes, and their reflections in the mutable things of the world below, the relation is "eternity." And considered as the relation between these mutable things, the relation is "time." Creation, or origination, is this very relation. Thus, the origination of the immutable Intelligences, or archetypes, is called "everlasting creation," the origination of the world of mutable beings as a whole is called "eternal creation," and the generation of mutable things within the world is called "temporal creation."

THE TEACHINGS OF MULLĀ ṢADRĀ

Mullā Ṣadrā superimposed Ibn al-ʿArabī's mystical thought (whose philosophic implications had already been exposed by a number of commentators) on the "Aristotelian"-illuminationist synthesis developed by Mīr Dāmād. Against his master, he argued with the Aristotelians for the priority of being (existence) over essence (form), which he called an abstraction; and, with Ibn al-ʿArabī, he argued for the "unity of being" within which beings differ only according to "priority

98

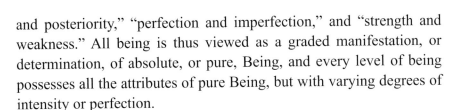

and posteriority," "perfection and imperfection," and "strength and weakness." All being is thus viewed as a graded manifestation, or determination, of absolute, or pure, Being, and every level of being possesses all the attributes of pure Being, but with varying degrees of intensity or perfection.

Mullā Ṣadrā considered his unique contribution to Islamic philosophy to be his doctrine of nature, which enabled him to assert that everything other than God and his knowledge—i.e., the entire corporeal world, including the heavenly bodies—is originated "eternally" as well as "temporally." This doctrine of nature is an elaboration of the last manifestation of what Ibn al-ʿArabī called "nature" or prime "matter" and is articulated on philosophic grounds and within the general framework of Aristotelian natural science and defended against every possible philosophic and theological objection.

Nature for Mullā Ṣadrā is the "substance" and "power" of all corporeal beings and the direct cause of their movement. Movement (and time, which measures it) is therefore not an accident of substance or an accompaniment of some of its accidents. It signifies the very change, renewal, and passing of being—itself being in constant "flow," or flux. The entire corporeal world, both the celestial spheres and the world of the elements, constantly renews itself. The "matter" of corporeal things has the power to become a new form at every instant; and the resulting matter–form complex is at every instant a new matter ready for, desiring, and moving toward another form. Human beings fail to observe this constant flux and movement in simple bodies not because of the endurance of the same form in them but because of the close similarity between their ever-new forms. What the philosophers call "movement" and "time" are not, as they believed, anchored in anything permanent—e.g., in what they call "nature," "substance," or "essence"; essence is permanent only in the mind, and nature and substance are

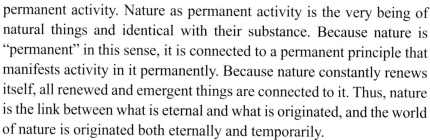

permanent activity. Nature as permanent activity is the very being of natural things and identical with their substance. Because nature is "permanent" in this sense, it is connected to a permanent principle that manifests activity in it permanently. Because nature constantly renews itself, all renewed and emergent things are connected to it. Thus, nature is the link between what is eternal and what is originated, and the world of nature is originated both eternally and temporarily.

Mullā Ṣadrā distinguishes this primary "movement-in-substance" (al-ḥarakah fī al-jawhar) from haphazard, compulsory, and other accidental movements that lack proper direction, impede the natural movement of substance, or reverse it. Movement-in-substance is not universal change or flux without direction, the product of conflict between two equally powerful principles, or a reflection of the nonbeing of the world of nature when measured against the world of permanent forms. It is, rather, the natural beings' innate desire to become more perfect, which directs this ceaseless self-renewal, self-origination, or self-emergence into a perpetual and irreversible flow upward in the scale of being—from the simplest elements to the human body–soul complex and the heavenly body–soul complex (both of which participate in the general instability, origination, and passing of being that characterizes the entire corporeal world). This flow upward, however, is by no means the end, for the indefinite "matter" (Ibn al-ʿArabī's "cloud" and the mystics' "created Truth") is the "substratum" of everything other than its Creator, the mysterious pure Truth. It "extends" beyond the body–soul complex to the Intelligences (divine names) that are Being's first, highest, and purest actualization or activity. This "extension" unites everything other than the Creator into a single continuum. The human body–soul complex and the heavenly body–soul complex are not moved externally by the Intelligences. Their movement is an extension of the process of self-perfection. Having reached the highest rank of order of substance in the corporeal world, they are now prepared, and still

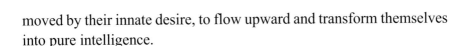

moved by their innate desire, to flow upward and transform themselves into pure intelligence.

IMPACT OF MODERNISM

The new wisdom lived on during the 18th and 19th centuries, conserving much of its vitality and strength but not cultivating new ground. It attracted able thinkers such as Shāh Walī Allāh of Delhi and Hādī Sabzevārī and became a regular part of the program of higher education in the cultural centres of the Ottoman Empire, Iran, and the Indian subcontinent, a status never achieved by the earlier tradition of Islamic philosophy. In collaboration with its close ally Persian mystical poetry, the new wisdom determined the intellectual outlook and spiritual mood of educated Muslims in the regions where Persian had become the dominant literary language.

The wholesale rejection of the new wisdom in the name of simple, robust, and more practical piety (which had been initiated by Ibn Taymiyyah and which continued to find exponents among jurists) made little impression on its devotees. To be taken seriously, reform had to come from their own ranks and be espoused by such thinkers as the eminent theologian and mystic of Muslim India Aḥmad Sirhindī (flourished 16th–17th centuries)—a reformer who spoke their language and attacked Ibn al-ʿArabī's "unity of being" only to defend an older, presumably more orthodox form of mysticism. Despite some impact, however, attempts of this kind remained isolated and were either ignored or reintegrated into the mainstream, until the coming of the modern reformers. The 19th- and 20th-century reformers Jamāl al-Dīn al-Afghānī, Muḥammad ʿAbduh, and Muḥammad Iqbāl were initially educated in this tradition, but they rebelled against it and advocated radical reforms.

The modernists attacked the new wisdom at its weakest point; that is, its social and political norms, its individualistic ethics, and its inability to speak intelligently about social, cultural, and political problems generated by a long period of intellectual isolation that was further complicated by the domination of the European powers. Unlike the earlier tradition of Islamic philosophy from al-Fārābī to Averroës, which had consciously cultivated political science and investigated the political dimension of philosophy and religion and the relation between philosophy and the community at large, the new wisdom from its inception lacked genuine interest in these questions, had no appreciation for political philosophy, and had only a benign toleration for the affairs of the world.

None of the reformers was a great political philosopher. They were concerned with reviving their nations' latent energies, urging them to free themselves from foreign domination, and impressing on them the need to reform their social and educational institutions. They also saw that all this required a total reorientation, which could not take place so long as the new wisdom remained not only the highest aim of a few solitary individuals but also a social and popular ideal as well. Yet, as late as 1917, Iqbāl found that "the present-day Muslim prefers to roam about aimlessly

Jamāl al-Dīn al-Afghānī (1838–1897) was a Muslim reformer whose belief in the potency of a revived Islamic civilization in the face of European domination significantly influenced the development of Muslim thought in the 19th and early 20th centuries.

in the valley of Hellenic-Persian mysticism, which teaches us to shut our eyes to the hard reality around, and to fix our gaze on what is described as 'illumination.'" His reaction was harsh: "To me this self-mystification, this nihilism, i.e., seeking reality where it does not exist, is a physiological symptom, giving me a clue to the decadence of the Muslim world."

To infuse new vitality in a society in which they were convinced religion must remain the focal point, the modern reformers advocated a return to the movements and masters of Islamic theology and philosophy antedating the new wisdom. They argued that these, rather than the "Persian incrustation of Islam," represented Islam's original and creative impulse. The modernists were attracted, in particular, to the views of the Mu'tazilah: affirmation of God's unity and denial of all similarity between him and created things; reliance on human reason; emphasis on human freedom; faith in human ability to distinguish between good and bad; and insistence on human responsibility to do good and fight against evil in private and public places. They were also impressed by the traditionalists' devotion to the original, uncomplicated forms of Islam and by their fighting spirit, and by the Ash'arīs' view of faith as an affair of the heart and their spirited defense of the Muslim community. In viewing the scientific and philosophic tradition of Eastern and Western Islam prior to the Tatar and Mongol invasions, they saw an irrefutable proof that true Islam stands for the liberation of the human spirit, promotes critical thought, and provides both the impetus to grapple with the temporal and the demonstration of how to set it in order. These ideas initiated what was to become a vast effort to recover, edit, and translate into the Muslim national languages works of earlier theologians and philosophers, which had been long neglected or known only indirectly through later accounts.

The modern reformers insisted, finally, that Muslims must be taught to understand the real meaning of what has happened in

103

Europe, which in effect means the understanding of modern science and philosophy, including modern social and political philosophies. Initially, this challenge became the task of the new universities in the Muslim world. In the latter part of the 20th century, however, the originally wide gap between the various programs of theological and philosophic studies in religious colleges and in modern universities narrowed considerably.

Chapter 5

Islamic Social and Ethical Principles

F ar from being strictly concerned with theology, the core teachings of Islam as embodied in the Qur'ān and various Hadith also address the social and political organization of the Muslim community. While such beliefs generally have manifested in a variety of ways depending on the surrounding culture and context of their expression, certain core principles bind all Islamic societies.

Family Life

A basic social teaching of Islam is the encouragement of marriage, and the Qur'ān regards celibacy definitely as something exceptional—to be resorted to only under economic stringency. Thus, monasticism as a way of life was severely criticized by the Qur'ān. With the appearance of Sufism (Islamic mysticism), however, many Sufis preferred celibacy, and some even regarded women as an evil distraction from piety, although marriage remained the normal practice also with Sufis.

Polygamy, which was practiced in pre-Islamic Arabia, was permitted by the Qur'ān, which, however, limited the number of simultaneous wives to four, and this permission was made dependent upon the condition that justice be done among co-wives. The Qur'ān even suggests that "you shall never be able to do

justice among women, no matter how much you desire." Medieval law and society, however, regarded this "justice" to be primarily a private matter between a husband and his wives, although the law did provide redress in cases of gross neglect of a wife. Right of divorce was also vested basically in the husband, who could unilaterally repudiate his wife, although the woman could also sue her husband for divorce before a court on certain grounds.

The virtue of chastity is regarded as of prime importance by Islam. The Qurʾān advanced its universal recommendation of marriage as a means to ensure a state of chastity (*iḥsān*), which is held to be induced by a single free wife. The Qurʾān states that those guilty of adultery are to be severely punished with 100 lashes. Tradition has intensified this injunction and has prescribed this punishment for unmarried persons, but married adulterers are to be stoned to death. A false accusation of adultery is punishable by 80 lashes.

The general ethic of the Qurʾān considers the marital bond to rest on "mutual love and mercy," and the spouses are said to be "each other's garments." The detailed laws of inheritance prescribed by the Qurʾān also tend to confirm the idea of a central family—husband, wife, and children, along with the husband's parents. Easy access to polygamy (although the normal practice in Islamic society has always been that of monogamy) and easy divorce on the part of the husband led, however, to frequent abuses in the family. In recent times, most Muslim countries have enacted legislation to tighten up marital relationships.

Rights of parents in terms of good treatment are stressed in Islam, and the Qurʾān extols filial piety, particularly tenderness to the mother, as an important virtue. A murderer of his father is automatically disinherited. The tendency of the Islamic ethic to strengthen the immediate family on the one hand and the community on the other at the expense of the extended family or tribe did not

Villagers clap along as a Muslim groom and bride perform a traditional dance at a wedding in Tālesh, Iran.

succeed, however. Muslim society, until the encroachments upon it of modernizing influences, has remained basically one composed of tribes or quasi-tribes. Despite urbanization, tribal affiliations offer the greatest resistance to change and development of a modern polity. So strong, indeed, has been the tribal ethos that, in most Muslim societies, daughters are not given their inheritance share prescribed by the sacred law in order to prevent disintegration of the joint family's patrimony.

The State

Because Islam draws no distinction between the religious and the temporal spheres of life, the Muslim state is by definition religious. The

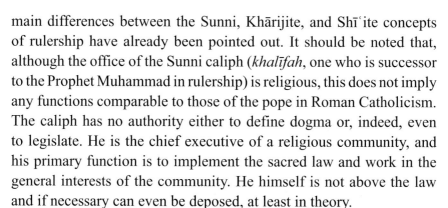

main differences between the Sunni, Khārijite, and Shī'ite concepts of rulership have already been pointed out. It should be noted that, although the office of the Sunni caliph (*khalīfah*, one who is successor to the Prophet Muhammad in rulership) is religious, this does not imply any functions comparable to those of the pope in Roman Catholicism. The caliph has no authority either to define dogma or, indeed, even to legislate. He is the chief executive of a religious community, and his primary function is to implement the sacred law and work in the general interests of the community. He himself is not above the law and if necessary can even be deposed, at least in theory.

Sunni political theory is essentially a product of circumstance—an after-the-fact rationalization of historical developments. Thus, between the Shī'ite legitimism that restricts rule to 'Alī's family and the Khārijite democratism that allowed rulership to anyone, even to "an Ethiopian slave," Sunnism held the position that "rule belonged to the Quraysh" (the Prophet's tribe)—the condition that actually existed. Again, in view of the extremes represented by the Khārijites, who demanded rebellion against what they considered to be unjust or impious rule, and Shī'ites, who raised the imam to a metaphysical plane of infallibility, Sunnis took the position that a ruler has to satisfy certain qualifications but that rule cannot be upset on small issues. Indeed, under the impact of civil wars started by the Khārijites, Sunnism drifted to more and more conformism and actual toleration of injustice.

The first step taken in this direction by the Sunnis was the enunciation that "one day of lawlessness is worse than 30 years of tyranny." This was followed by the principle that "Muslims must obey even a tyrannical ruler." Soon, however, the sultan (ruler) was declared to be "shadow of God on earth." No doubt, the principle was also adopted—and insisted upon—that "there can be no obedience to the ruler in disobedience of God"; but there is no

denying the fact that the Sunni doctrine came more and more to be heavily weighted on the side of political conformism. This change is also reflected in the principles of legitimacy. Whereas early Islam had confirmed the pre-Islamic democratic Arab principle of rule by consultation (*shūrā*) and some form of democratic election of the leader, those practices soon gave way to dynastic rule with the advent of the Umayyads. The *shūrā* was not developed into any institutionalized form and was, indeed, soon discarded. Soon the principle of "might is right" came into being, and later theorists frankly acknowledged that actual possession of effective power is one method of the legitimization of power.

In spite of this development, the ruler could not become absolute, because a basic restraint was placed upon him by the Sharīʿah law under which he held his authority and which he dutifully was bound to execute and defend. When, in the latter half of the 16th century, the Mughal emperor Akbar in India wanted to arrogate to himself the right of administrative–legal absolutism, the strong reaction of the orthodox thwarted his attempt. In general, the *ʿulamāʾ* (religious scholars) jealously upheld the sovereign position of the Sharīʿah against the political authority.

The effective shift of power from the caliph to the sultan was, again, reflected in the redefinition of the functions of the caliph. It was conceded that, if the caliph administered through *wazīrs* (viziers or ministers) or subordinate rulers (*amīrs*), it was not necessary for him to embody all the physical, moral, and intellectual virtues theoretically insisted upon earlier. In practice, however, the caliph was no more than a titular head from the middle of the 10th century onward, when real power passed to self-made and adventurous *amīrs* and sultans, who merely used the caliph's name for legitimacy.

EDUCATION

Ottoman sultan Abdülhamid II (1842–1918), who ruled from 1876 to 1909, embodied the power associated with the position of sultan. In modern times, the assumption of such titles is generally not supported by a true religious consensus among Muslims, but rather reflects political conditions in a given country or community.

Muslim educational activity began in the 8th century, primarily in order to disseminate the teaching of the Qur'ān and the Sunnah of the Prophet. The first task in this endeavour was to record the oral traditions and collect the written manuscripts. This information was systematically organized in the 2nd century AH, and in the following century a sound corpus was agreed upon. This vast activity of "seeking knowledge" (*talab al-'ilm*) resulted in the creation of specifically Arab sciences of tradition, history, and literature.

When the introduction of the Greek sciences—philosophy, medicine, and mathematics—created a formidable body of lay knowledge, a creative reaction on the traditional religious base resulted in the rationalist theological movement of the Mu'tazilah. Based on that Greek legacy, from the 9th to the 12th century CE a brilliant philosophical movement flowered and presented a challenge to orthodoxy on the issues of the eternity of the world, the doctrine of revelation, and the status of the Sharī'ah.

THE CALIPHATE

The Caliphate refers to the political-religious state comprising the Muslim community and the lands and peoples under its dominion in the centuries following the death of Muhammad. Ruled by a caliph (Arabic *khalīfah,* "successor"), who held temporal and sometimes a degree of spiritual authority, the empire of the Caliphate grew rapidly through conquest during its first two centuries to include most of Southwest Asia, North Africa, and Spain. Dynastic struggles later brought about the Caliphate's decline, and it ceased to exist with the Mongol destruction of Baghdad in 1258.

The concept of the caliphate took on new significance in the 18th century as an instrument of statecraft in the declining Ottoman Empire. Facing the erosion of their military and political power and territorial losses inflicted in a series of wars with European rivals, the Ottoman sultans, who had occasionally styled themselves as caliphs since the 14th century, began to stress their claim to leadership of the Islamic community. This served both as means of retaining some degree of influence over Muslim populations in formerly Ottoman lands and as means of bolstering Ottoman legitimacy within the empire. The caliphate was abolished in 1924, following the dissolution of the Ottoman Empire and the rise of the Turkish Republic.

In the 20th century the reestablishment of the caliphate, although occasionally invoked by Islamists as a symbol of global Islamic unity, was of no practical interest for mainstream Islamist groups such as the Muslim Brotherhood in Egypt. It did, however, figure prominently in the rhetoric of violent extremist groups such as al-Qaeda. In June 2014 an insurgent group known as the Islamic State in Iraq and the Levant (ISIL; also known as the Islamic State in Iraq and Syria [ISIS] and the Islamic State [IS]), which had

(continued on the next page)

(continued from the previous page)

taken control of areas of eastern Syria and western Iraq, declared the establishment of a caliphate with the group's leader Abu Bakr al-Baghdadi as caliph. Outside of extremist circles, the group's claim was widely rejected.

The orthodox met the challenges positively by formulating the religious dogma. At the same time, however, for fear of heresies, they began to draw a sharp distinction between religious and secular sciences. The custodians of the Sharī'ah developed an unsympathetic attitude toward the secular disciplines and excluded them from the curriculum of the *madrasah* (college) system.

Their exclusion from the Sunni system of education proved fatal, not only for those disciplines but, in the long run, for religious thought in general because of the lack of intellectual challenge and stimulation. A typical madrasah curriculum included logic (which was considered necessary as an "instrumental" science for the formal correctness of thinking procedure), Arabic literature, law, Hadith, Qur'ān commentary, and theology. Despite sporadic criticism from certain quarters, the madrasah system remained impervious to change.

One important feature of Muslim education was that primary education (which consisted of Qur'ān reading, writing, and rudimentary arithmetic) did not feed candidates to institutions of higher education, and the two remained separate. In higher education, emphasis was on books rather than on subjects and on commentaries rather than on original works. This, coupled with the habit of learning by rote (which was developed from the basically traditional character of knowledge that encouraged learning more than thinking), impoverished intellectual creativity still further.

Despite these grave shortcomings, however, the madrasah produced one important advantage. Through the uniformity of its religio-legal content, it gave the *'ulamā'* the opportunity to effect that overall cohesiveness and unity of thought and purpose that, despite

Madrasah at the Jāmiʿ Masjid ("Great Mosque") in Shrirangapattana, Karnataka, India.

great variations in local Muslim cultures, has become a palpable feature of the world Muslim community. This uniformity has withstood even the serious tension created against the seats of formal learning by Sufism through its peculiar discipline and its own centres.

In contrast to the Sunni attitude toward it, philosophy continued to be seriously cultivated among the Shīʿites, even though it developed a strong religious character. Indeed, philosophy has enjoyed an unbroken tradition in Iran down to the present and has produced some highly original thinkers. Both the Sunni and the Shīʿite medieval systems of learning, however, have come face to face with the greatest challenge of all—the impact of modern education and thought.

Organization of education developed naturally in the course of time. Evidence exists of small schools already established in the first century of Islam that were devoted to reading, writing, and instruction in the Qurʾān. These schools of "primary" education were called *kuttābs*. The well-known governor of Iraq at the beginning of the 8th century, the ruthless al-Ḥajjāj, had been a schoolteacher in his early career. When higher learning in the form of tradition grew in the 8th and 9th centuries, it was centred around learned men to whom students travelled from far and near and from whom they obtained a certificate (*ijāzah*) to teach what they had learned. Through the munificence of rulers and princes, large private and public libraries were built, and schools and colleges arose.

In the early 9th century a significant incentive to learning came from the translations made of scientific and philosophical works from the Greek (and partly Sanskrit) at the famous *bayt al-ḥikmah* ("house of wisdom") at Baghdad, which was officially sponsored by the caliph al-Ma'mūn. The Fāṭimid caliph al-Ḥākim set up a *dār al-ḥikmah* ("hall of wisdom") in Cairo in the 10th–11th centuries. With the advent of the Seljuq Turks, the famous vizier Niẓām al-Mulk created an important college at Baghdad, devoted to Sunni learning, in the latter half of the 11th century. One of the world's oldest surviving universities, al-Azhar at Cairo, was originally established by the Fāṭimids, but Saladin (Ṣalāḥ al-Dīn al-Ayyūbī), after ousting the Fāṭimids, consecrated it to Sunni learning in the 12th century. Throughout subsequent centuries, colleges and quasi-universities (called *madrasah* or *dār al-'ulūm*) arose throughout the Muslim world from Spain (whence philosophy and science were transmitted to the Latin West) across Central Asia to India.

In Turkey a new style of madrasah came into existence; it had four wings, for the teaching of the four schools of Sunni law. Professorial chairs were endowed in large colleges by princes and governments, and residential students were supported by college endowment funds. A myriad of smaller centres of learning were endowed by private donations.

CULTURAL DIVERSITY

Underneath the legal and creedal unity, the world of Islam harbours a tremendous diversity of cultures, particularly in the outlying regions. The expansion of Islam can be divided into two broad periods. In the first period of the Arab conquests, the assimilative activity of the conquering religion was far-reaching. Although Persia resurrected its own language and a measure of its national culture after the first three centuries of Islam, its culture and language had come under heavy Arab influence. Only after Ṣafavid rule installed Shī'ism as a distinctive creed in the 16th century did Persia regain a kind of religious autonomy. The language of religion and thought, however, continued to be Arabic.

In the second period, the spread of Islam was not conducted by the state with 'ulamā' influence but was largely the work of Sufi missionaries. The Sufis, because of their latitudinarianism, compromised with local customs and beliefs and left a great deal of the pre-Islamic legacy in every region intact. Thus, among the Central Asian Turks, shamanistic practices were absorbed, while in Africa the holy man and his *barakah* (an influence supposedly causing material and spiritual well-being) are survivors from the older cults. In India there are large areas geographically distant from the Muslim religio-political centre of power in which customs are still Hindu and even pre-Hindu and in which people worship a motley of saints and deities in common with the Hindus. The custom of *suttee*, under which a widow burned herself alive along with her dead husband, persisted in India even among some Muslims until late into the Mughal period. The 18th- and 19th-century reform movements exerted themselves to "purify" Islam of these accretions and superstitions.

Ramadan is celebrated at the Masjid Istiqlāl ("Great Mosque") in Palembang, Indonesia.

Indonesia affords a striking example of this phenomenon. Because Islam reached there late and soon thereafter came under European colonialism, the Indonesian society has retained its pre-Islamic worldview beneath an overlay of Islamic practices. It keeps its customary law (called *adat*) at the expense of the Sharī'ah; many of its tribes are still matriarchal; and culturally the Hindu epics *Ramayana* and *Mahabharata* hold a high position in national life. Since the 19th century, however, orthodox Islam has gained steadily in strength because of fresh contacts with the Middle East.

Apart from regional diversity, the main internal division within Islamic society is brought about by urban and village life. Islam originally grew up in the two cities of Mecca and Medina, and, as it expanded, its peculiar ethos appears to have developed in urban areas. Culturally, it came under a heavy Persian influence in Iraq, where the Arabs learned the ways and style of life of their conquered people, who were culturally superior to them. The custom of veiling women (which originally arose as a sign of aristocracy

PURDAH

Purdah (in Hindi, Parda: "screen," or "veil") is the practice that was inaugurated by Muslims and later adopted by various Hindus, especially in India, involving the seclusion of women from public observation by means of concealing clothing (including the veil) and by the use of high-walled enclosures, screens, and curtains within the home.

The practice of purdah is said to have originated in the Persian culture and to have been acquired by the Muslims during the Arab conquest of what is now Iraq in the 7th century CE. Muslim domination of northern India in turn influenced the practice of Hinduism, and purdah became usual among the Hindu upper classes

(continued on the next page)

(continued from the previous page)

of northern India. During the British hegemony in India, purdah observance was strictly adhered to and widespread among the highly conscious Muslim minority. Since then, purdah has largely disappeared in Hindu practice, though the seclusion and veiling of women is practiced to a greater or lesser degree in many Islamic countries.

Some modern Islamic regimes have insisted on the strict veiling of women in public. The enveloping cloaks worn by women for this purpose are similar to one another and often incorporate a mesh panel through which women may peer at the world outside. The most common names for such veils are *burka*, *ḥijāb*, *niqāb*, *chador*, *chādar*, *çarşaf*, *chadri*, and *tcharchaf*.

but later served the purpose of segregating women from men—the *purdah*), for example, was acquired in Iraq.

Another social trait derived from outside cultures was the disdain for agriculture and manual labour in general. Because the people of the town of Medina were mainly agriculturists, this disdain could not have been initially present. In general, Islam came to appropriate a strong feudal ethic from the peoples it conquered. Also, because the Muslims generally represented the administrative and military aristocracy and because the learned class (the *'ulamā'*) was an essential arm of the state, the higher culture of Islam became urban-based.

This city orientation explains and also underlines the traditional cleavage between the orthodox Islam of the *'ulamā'* and the folk Islam espoused by the Sufi orders of the countryside. In the modern period, the advent of education and rapid industrialization threatened to make this cleavage still wider. With the rise of a strong and widespread fundamentalist movement in the second half of the 20th century, this dichotomy was decreased.

CONCLUSION

Islam has become a routine topic of political commentary and news coverage as extremist violence plagues entire regions of the globe at the hands of religious terrorist groups such as the Islamic State in Iraq and the Levant (ISIL) and Boko Haram. As such, the true doctrines of Islam often have been conflated for the extremist practices of such groups, and many of those unfamiliar with Islam are wary of and even prejudiced against Muslims. In September 2016, the *New York Times* reported that hate crimes against Muslims in the United States had risen 78 percent over the course of 2015.

When approached objectively, Islam can be seen for what it truly is: a peaceful religion whose core values emphasize prayer, devotion to God, and community. Once the true foundations of Islam are understood, the stereotypes and stigmas surrounding the religion disappear. Furthermore, Islam can in no way be considered a singular, global entity, but rather a diverse network of cultures and religious sects that, while sharing many common practices and beliefs, are almost always influenced by their specific context.

The value of understanding Islam is clear. By becoming familiar with the foundations of the religion and its many intricacies and interpretations, it is easier to erase misperceptions and truly approach one of the world's great religions.

GLOSSARY

ABHOR To dislike (someone or something) very much.

AH Anno hegirae; used to indicate that a time division falls within the Islamic era.

CALIPH A successor of Muhammad as temporal and spiritual head of Islam, used as a title.

CANONICAL Of or relating to the books that are considered to be part of a religion's official text.

CATHOLICITY Liberality of sentiments or views.

CONCOMITANT Happening at the same time as something else.

CORPOREAL Having or consisting of a physical body or form.

DOXOGRAPHY Study of and commentary on ancient Greek philosophers.

GENUFLECTION The act of kneeling and then rising again as an act of respect.

HEGEMONY Influence or control over another country, a group of people, etc.

HERETICAL Of, relating to, or characterized by a belief or opinion that does not agree with the official belief of a particular religion.

HISTORIOGRAPHY The writing of history.

INCULCATE To cause (something) to be learned by (someone) by repeating it again and again.

INTERNECINE Of, relating to, or involving conflict within a group.

JURISPRUDENCE The study of law.

KA'BAH A small stone building in the court of the Great Mosque at Mecca that contains a sacred black stone and is the goal of Islamic pilgrimage and the point toward which Muslims turn in praying.

MANDAEAN A member of a Gnostic sect that regards John the Baptist as the Messiah and that is found in regions of the lower Tigris and Euphrates.

MANICHAEISM A syncretistic religious dualism originating in Persia by the prophet Mani, which teaches that a cosmic conflict exists between a good realm of light and an evil realm of darkness.

MANIFOLD Many and various.

MONOTHEISM The doctrine or belief that there is only one God.

OSCILLATION The act of changing from one belief, feeling, etc., to an opposite one.

PILGRIMAGE A journey to a holy place.

POLYTHEISM Belief in or worship of more than one god.

PROSTRATION The act of assuming a stretched-out position with face on the ground in adoration or submission.

PUTATIVE Commonly accepted or supposed.

REPUDIATE To refuse to accept or support (something) or to reject (something or someone).

SCHISM A division among the members of a group that occurs because they disagree on something.

SECTARIAN Relating to religious or political sects and the differences between them.

SUBSERVIENT Very willing to obey someone else.

UNADULTERATED Pure, whole, and uncorrupted.

VICE-REGENT The deputy to one who rules or reigns.

VIZIER A high executive officer of various Muslim countries.

ZOROASTRIANISM A Persian religion founded in the sixth century BCE by the prophet Zoroaster, promulgated in the Avesta, and characterized by worship of a supreme god Ahura Mazda, who requires good deeds for help in his cosmic struggle against the evil spirit Ahriman.

BIBLIOGRAPHY

GENERAL WORKS

Cambridge History of Islam, vol. 2, part 8 (1970, reissued 1977, vol. 2B), provides an excellent survey. Marshall G.S. Hodgson, *The Venture of Islam*, 3 vol. (1974), is a major study of the religion and civilization. R.M. Savory (ed.), *Introduction to Islamic Civilization* (1976), collects scholarly articles on Islamic history, religion, literature, language, and other topics. Bernard Lewis (ed.), *The World of Islam: Faith, People, Culture* (1976; also published as *Islam and the Arab World*), collects articles on various aspects of Islamic culture, and his *Islam: From the Prophet Muhammad to the Capture of Constantinople*, 2 vol. (1974), is composed of translations of original sources. W. Montgomery Watt, *The Majesty That Was Islam: The Islamic World, 661–1100* (1974), presents a concise history of the rise and decline of the Islamic empire. Hamilton A.R. Gibb, *Mohammedanism*, 2nd ed. (1953, reissued with revisions 1969), is a concise account of the development of Islam. Louis Gardet, *Mohammedanism*, trans. by William Burridge (1961), is a systematic presentation of Islam, with religious insight. Fazlur Rahman, *Islam*, 2nd ed. (1979), provides a historical and systematic interpretation of Islam, and his *Islamic Methodology in History* (1965) presents a critical appraisal of the development of Sunnah, *ijmā‘*, and *ijtihād*. Reubin Levy, *An Introduction to the Sociology of Islam* (1930–), is a useful account of the development of Islamic society and institutions. John W. Bagnole, *Cultures of the Islamic Middle East* (1978), is an annotated guide to 402 English-language readings.

EDUCATION

Arthur S. Tritton, *Materials on Muslim Education in the Middle Ages* (1957), is an informative, useful compilation. Bayard Dodge, *Muslim Education in Medieval Times* (1962), provides a useful sketch.

POLITICAL THEORY AND INSTITUTIONS

Erwin I.J. Rosenthal, *Political Thought in Medieval Islam* (1958), is a good general survey of the subject.

ISLAMIC ARTS

In view of the wealth of descriptive treatments, rather than theory, it is difficult to point to a single source. K.A.C. Creswell, *A Bibliography of the Architecture, Arts and Crafts of Islam to 1st Jan. 1960* (1961), and *Supplement, Jan. 1960 to Jan. 1972* (1973), contain all the necessary references, and his *Early Muslim Architecture*, 2nd ed. (1969), is also useful; as is American University at Cairo, Center for Arabic Studies, *Studies in Islamic Art and Architecture in Honor of Professor K.A.C. Creswell* (1965).

Hamilton A.R. Gibb, *Arabic Literature: An Introduction*, 2nd ed. (1974), is a probing survey of 1,500 years of literature. Salih J. Altoma, *Modern Arabic Literature* (1975), provides a bibliography of 850 general and scholarly works covering 1800–1970.

THEOLOGY AND PHILOSOPHY

Franz Rosenthal (ed.), *The Classical Heritage in Islam*, trans. from the German by Emile Marmorstein and Jenny Marmorstein (1975); and Richard Walzer, *Greek into Arabic: Essays on Islamic Philosophy* (1962, reissued 1970), deal with the Greek and Hellenistic background and its appropriation. Parviz Morewedge (ed.), *Islamic Philosophical Theology* (1979), is a major contribution by nine internationally known authorities written for advanced students. W. Montgomery Watt, *The*

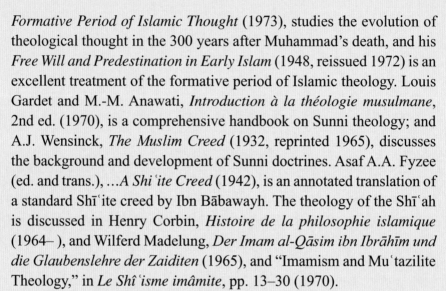

Formative Period of Islamic Thought (1973), studies the evolution of theological thought in the 300 years after Muhammad's death, and his *Free Will and Predestination in Early Islam* (1948, reissued 1972) is an excellent treatment of the formative period of Islamic theology. Louis Gardet and M.-M. Anawati, *Introduction à la théologie musulmane*, 2nd ed. (1970), is a comprehensive handbook on Sunni theology; and A.J. Wensinck, *The Muslim Creed* (1932, reprinted 1965), discusses the background and development of Sunni doctrines. Asaf A.A. Fyzee (ed. and trans.), *...A Shi'ite Creed* (1942), is an annotated translation of a standard Shī'ite creed by Ibn Bābawayh. The theology of the Shī'ah is discussed in Henry Corbin, *Histoire de la philosophie islamique* (1964–), and Wilferd Madelung, *Der Imam al-Qāsim ibn Ibrāhīm und die Glaubenslehre der Zaiditen* (1965), and "Imamism and Mu'tazilite Theology," in *Le Shî'isme imâmite*, pp. 13–30 (1970).

M.M. Sharif (ed.), *A History of Muslim Philosophy*, 2 vol. (1963–66), is a comprehensive collective work on the history of Islamic philosophy and related subjects that is especially useful for the later medieval and modern periods. Majid Fakhry, *A History of Islamic Philosophy* (1970), is a general history. Fazlur Rahman discusses the development of the later synthesis between mysticism and philosophy in "Dream, Imagination, and 'Ālam al-Mithāl," *Islamic Studies*, vol. 3, no. 2, pp. 167–180 (June 1964), in the introduction to *Selected Letters of Shaikh Aḥmad Sirhindī* (1968), and in "The Eternity of the World and the Heavenly Bodies in Post-Avicennan Philosophy," in George F. Hourani (ed.), *Essays on Islamic Philosophy and Science* (1975), a collection representing recent trends in interpreting Islamic philosophy.

ISLAMIC MYTH AND LEGEND

Tor Andrae, *Die Person Muhammeds in Lehre und Glauben seiner Gemeinde* (1917), treats the development of Muhammad-mysticism.

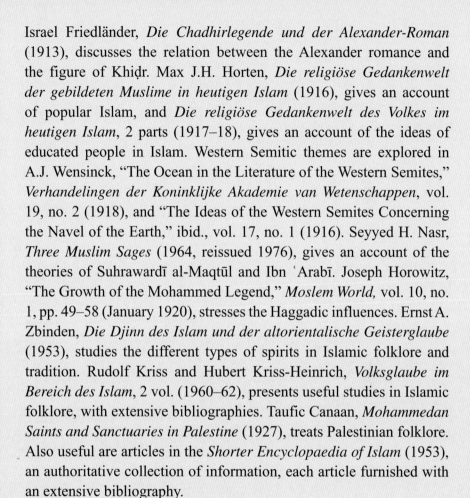

Israel Friedländer, *Die Chadhirlegende und der Alexander-Roman* (1913), discusses the relation between the Alexander romance and the figure of Khiḍr. Max J.H. Horten, *Die religiöse Gedankenwelt der gebildeten Muslime in heutigen Islam* (1916), gives an account of popular Islam, and *Die religiöse Gedankenwelt des Volkes im heutigen Islam*, 2 parts (1917–18), gives an account of the ideas of educated people in Islam. Western Semitic themes are explored in A.J. Wensinck, "The Ocean in the Literature of the Western Semites," *Verhandelingen der Koninklijke Akademie van Wetenschappen*, vol. 19, no. 2 (1918), and "The Ideas of the Western Semites Concerning the Navel of the Earth," ibid., vol. 17, no. 1 (1916). Seyyed H. Nasr, *Three Muslim Sages* (1964, reissued 1976), gives an account of the theories of Suhrawardī al-Maqtūl and Ibn ʿArabī. Joseph Horowitz, "The Growth of the Mohammed Legend," *Moslem World,* vol. 10, no. 1, pp. 49–58 (January 1920), stresses the Haggadic influences. Ernst A. Zbinden, *Die Djinn des Islam und der altorientalische Geisterglaube* (1953), studies the different types of spirits in Islamic folklore and tradition. Rudolf Kriss and Hubert Kriss-Heinrich, *Volksglaube im Bereich des Islam*, 2 vol. (1960–62), presents useful studies in Islamic folklore, with extensive bibliographies. Taufic Canaan, *Mohammedan Saints and Sanctuaries in Palestine* (1927), treats Palestinian folklore. Also useful are articles in the *Shorter Encyclopaedia of Islam* (1953), an authoritative collection of information, each article furnished with an extensive bibliography.

INDEX